At Issue

Drug Testing

Other books in the At Issue series:

At Issue

Drug Testing

Cindy Mur, Book Editor

GREENHAVEN PRESS

An imprint of Thomson Gale, a part of The Thomson Corporation

Detroit • New York • San Francisco • San Diego • New Haven, Conn. • Waterville, Maine • London • Munich

LIBRARY OF CONGRESS CATALOGING-IN-PUBLICATION DATA

Drug testing / Cindy Mur, book editor.
    p. cm. -- (At Issue)
    Includes bibliographical references and index.
    ISBN 0-7377-3093-5 (lib. bdg.: alk. paper) -- ISBN 0-7377-3094-3
(pbk.: alk. paper)
    1. Drug testing--United States. I. At issue (San Diego, Calif.)
    HV5823.5.U5D76 2006
    362.29'16407973--dc22
                             2005044723

Printed in the United States of America
10 9 8 7 6 5 4 3 2 1

MAR 2007

Contents

Introduction

Employers, schools, and athletic organizations all employ drug testing as a means of detecting and preventing drug use. Many employers utilize a testing program to detect recreational drug use as a means of screening potential employees or of maintaining a drug-free workplace. Athletes may try to enhance their performance with drugs such as steroids, so all professional athletic organizations in the United States as well as the Olympic Games use random drug testing as a means of identifying and deterring drug use. Lastly, schools employ drug testing to prevent both recreational and performance-enhancing drug use among students or to identify an individual student's drug problem.

There are five primary ways of drug testing used today: urine tests, saliva tests, follicle tests, blood tests, and sweat patches. The most common and yet most disputed test is the urine test. Urine collection methods may vary, as some organizations will watch an individual provide the sample as a means of verifying its integrity, while others, especially schools, will allow some privacy behind a bathroom stall door. Most samples are collected in specimen containers and sent to a lab for testing, although some new tests allow immediate results. Standard urine tests for recreational drugs check for marijuana, cocaine, methamphetamines, opiates such as heroin and morphine, benzodiazepines such as valium, and PCP. Athletic organizations use urine tests to check for substances like human growth hormones (HGH), which help build muscle mass and promote bone growth, as well as testosterone, synthetic THG (tetrahydrogestrinone), and other anabolic steroids.

Many believe that drug testing is an effective approach, along with education programs and criminal prosecution, to deter illegal drug use. One factor in determining whether drug testing can help prevent drug use is whether drug tests work effectively—particularly urine tests. This has become a hotly contested topic between those who support drug testing and those who criticize its value.

While the best urine tests are improving, critics say the cheapest and therefore most common are error-prone. As journalist Dana Hawkins states in his article "Tests on Trial" in *U.S. News & World Report,* "Studies of the cheapest of these tests ... show they give the right answer as little as one third of the time." The ways to purposefully "cheat" the test are numerous. Urine providers can simply drink a lot of water beforehand or add toilet water to dilute results. They can also use urine-altering substances such as masking agents and detoxicants. One detoxicant is a urine additive called "the Randomizer," which, when added to a urine sample, is said to remove all traces of a toxin. Those tested can also purchase warmed, "clean" urine—urine that is body temperature and free of any drugs—to substitute for their own drug-tainted sample. One example of this is a product called "the Urinator" that consists of a short tube attached to a battery-heated plastic bag. The user fills the bag with "clean" urine before testing, and it is warmed to body temperature by the apparatus. "The Whizzinator" works the same as the Urinator but replaces the tube with a prosthetic penis in case a male participant is watched during urination.

Some urine adulterants can be found in the home. In a 2003 article in *Medical Laboratory Observer,* Amitava Dasgupta notes that "household chemicals, such as bleach, acid, vinegar, lemon juice, eye drops and table salt are routinely used to beat drug tests." These items can be added to urine as a way of changing results or masking urine contents. Common foods and medications can produce false positive results as well. Marc D. Greenwood, an emergency medical technician, stated in a 2003 article in *Fire Chief* that

Robitussin [a cough suppressant] and diet pills can produce a false positive for amphetamines; ibuprofen and various antibiotics can duplicate marijuana; the combination of a kidney infection and diabetes can cause an individual to test positive for cocaine; migraine medications and anti-depressants can mimic LSD; and poppy seed consumption can give a positive reading for opiates.

Lastly, those critical of drug testing for athletes say that urine tests for drugs like anabolic steroids work well, but that steroid levels may fluctuate in the body and can vary from one person to another. As a result, authorities cannot agree on the point at which someone can be considered "using" steroids. In addition, urine tests have a short window in which to catch steroid use. Athletes can therefore take steroids during training to bulk up in advance of competition and then stop before the event with little worry of being caught. Opponents of drug testing for athletes also believe that laboratories cannot keep up with innovations because new steroidal compounds are continually being created by scientists.

Overall, critics of urine testing find that the number of ways to alter or circumvent urine tests, both purposefully and accidentally, make them too unreliable to be an effective tool for detecting drug use.

Proponents of drug testing challenge these criticisms. They state that methods are available to check whether a urine sample has been adulterated. In a 2003 article in *HR Magazine,* Laura Shelton, executive director of the Drug and Alcohol Testing Industry Association, was quoted as saying, "As adulterant companies come out with new products, labs test to detect what it is they're using to mask the drug." She states that lab employees monitor periodicals like *High Times* to keep up on the latest adulterant products. To check for contaminated samples, schools and other organizations need only ask that their lab test specimens for validity. Shelton suggests that an experienced lab can detect fraud by inspecting the sample for dilution as well as "smell, color, temperature, floating particles or foaming."

Some testing agencies use specific methods in sampling that discourage attempts to circumvent a urine test. For example, David Feinstein, a certified medical review officer with Industrial Health Care, said in a 2001 article in *American Salesman* that they used special collection products: "There is a temperature gauge on the side of the [urine sample] cup that allows us to make sure the sample registers between 90 and 100 degrees. Some of the mail order houses sell warmers which bring the fake sample up to temperature, but the pads either heat the sample too much or too little. Either way, we can tell." He also indicated that the water is turned off in the bathroom and the toilet water is colored blue to discourage sample dilution. If it appears that the sample has been diluted because the individual being tested drank a lot of water beforehand, the lab reschedules the test and sends that person home. When questioned about masking agents, Feinstein asserts that "Some chemicals cause irregular readings in the tests, but never give a false result."

Proponents of drug testing also say that labs are improving their detection capabilities for new steroidal drugs. Although the World Anti-Doping Agency struggles to keep up with the introduction of new products that enhance athletic performance, it employs testing year-round and can suddenly drop in on an athlete to take a sample—thereby catching someone who may be using an illegal drug in advance of competition.

The viability of all drug tests goes to the heart of the debate about drug testing. While there is spirited discussion concerning other types of tests—follicle, sweat, saliva, or blood tests—the debate surrounding urine testing captures the essence of the dialogue: the increasingly varied methods of drug users to circumvent tests versus the testers' technological ability to catch them. Scientific advances for both drug testers and drug test cheaters may mean that the race to catch those who use illegal drugs is a never-ending one. The authors in *At Issue: Drug Testing* debate the issues surrounding drug tests, privacy rights, costs (both financial and personal), and the overall effectiveness of drug testing programs.

1

Drug Testing Creates a Better Workplace Environment

Norm Brodsky

Norm Brodsky is an entrepreneur who owns six businesses, including a three-time Inc. 500 company. He is also a columnist for Inc. *magazine; his features include "Hiring Salespeople" and "Pennies from Heaven," the latter of which discusses employee retention techniques.*

Instituting a random drug testing policy in the workplace helps to reduce accidents and theft, creating a safer environment for all employees. In addition, testing all potential employees reduces the likelihood of hiring drug users who will probably not be able to perform at optimal levels. Employers may find that their insurance rates and workers' compensation costs decrease after instituting a drug testing policy. In some instances, drug testing in the workplace can encourage employees to live a drug-free life.

Often, I've found, you do something in business for one reason and only later discover that your decision has had ramifications you never imagined. With luck, they'll be good ones. That's been my experience with drug testing, which I began doing somewhat reluctantly [in 1998].

I knew we had a problem in our warehouse at the time. We'd heard rumors about marijuana being bought and sold on our premises. We'd also seen a marked increase in petty theft and minor accidents, which I suspected was related to drug use. People were running forklift trucks into walls and dropping skids of boxes onto the floor as they were being moved from one spot to another. Items would disappear from the shipments of goods that we kept in the warehouse for customers of our trucking business. I couldn't blame all of the problems on drug use, but I felt certain that it was a contributing factor.

Still, I hesitated to start drug testing. Part of my reluctance, I suppose, was a subconscious fear of feeling hypocritical. Like other members of my generation, I'd tried marijuana in my youth, and I'd be lying if I said I didn't inhale. When the testing issue arose, I had reservations about punishing people for doing something I'd also done at their age. In addition, I knew that drug testing could result in our having to let some employees go—maybe even some good, long-term employees—at a time when the growing labor shortage was making hiring increasingly difficult. That seemed likely to cost us a substantial amount of time and money—not to mention emotional anguish—over and above the cost of the testing itself. But I eventually decided that we had to go forward anyway, mainly because of the accidents. No one had been seriously injured, but I knew our luck would run out sooner or later.

A New Drug Testing Policy

So, after consulting with some experts we'd brought in to help us, we announced our new policy. Henceforward we would test all job applicants for use of illegal drugs and hire only those whose results came back negative. As for our current employees, we wanted to give people using drugs a chance to clean themselves up. Marijuana, we explained, would show up in urine samples for at least a month after use. Other drugs passed through the body's system more quickly. Accordingly, we would wait 45 to 60 days before beginning testing. Thereafter we would test everyone in the company, including me, my wife, my daughter, the other executives—everyone.

The tests would be random and would not be announced in advance. People who tested positive for drugs other than marijuana would be terminated immediately. Those who tested positive for marijuana use only would be given a second chance. After another 45-day waiting period, we'd do a second round of tests. Employees who failed both tests would be let go.

The drug testing did work. The accident rate declined, as did the incidence of petty theft.

Despite the warning, we were in for a shock. In the first few days of testing, half of the samples from current employees came back positive. You can imagine how we felt about the prospect of replacing 50% of our 130-person work force. We decided to slow down the testing, so that we'd have time to find the new people we'd need.

I had hopes for the employees who flunked the first test. Before the second round began, I asked several people if they were ready. Everybody said, "Oh, yeah, I'm clean." In the end, though, only one of them passed the second test, a young man named Bruce Howard. Although we offered the others drug treatment and a chance to reapply for a job, we got no takers. Overall, we wound up losing about 25% of our work force—fewer than we'd feared, but a significant number nonetheless.

The Benefits of Drug Testing

Yet the drug testing did work. The accident rate declined, as did the incidence of petty theft. Even more gratifying was the response of the employees who remained: They thanked us. They said they felt safer. Only then did I begin to appreciate the real importance of having a drug-free company. It wasn't just about reducing our liability, or even keeping someone from getting hurt, as much as we wanted to do both. It was also about creating a better working environment for the other employees, the ones on whom we depend most heavily, the people we absolutely must figure out how to keep.

And on top of that, we got a bonus. Our drug-testing program made us more attractive to insurers, allowing us to move our policies to a better provider. Over time, moreover, a lower accident rate would translate into lower workers' comp costs. . . .

Since then, we've continued to do random drug testing inside the company, in addition to testing all of our new hires. More than 75% of the latter group flunk the test, a result I find disturbing. I like to think that we're offering people an opportunity to have a better life, and it's extremely disappointing when they turn down the opportunity.

A Test Case

Consider the case of an intelligent, well-spoken, clean-cut young woman we wanted to hire as our executive secretary. She'd come to us through a reputable employment agency that had checked out all of her references. She had a great resume, and she impressed everyone in our company who spent time with her. I was the last person to interview her, and she impressed me, as well. In the course of our discussion, I mentioned that we drug test all new hires. She didn't bat an eye. Mainly she wanted to know the length of her lunch break. I told her it was 45 minutes. "Good," she said. "I need that time for myself."

"No problem," I said.

The next day we called the agency and said we intended to hire her. Someone from the agency called her with the news. She was thrilled. "They'll do the drug test tomorrow," the agent said.

There was a brief silence on the other end of the line. "They really do drug tests?" the job candidate asked. "That could be a problem."

"Why?" asked the agent.

"Because I won't pass," the young woman said. She explained that she was addicted to crack cocaine. She smoked it every day at lunch. That's why she needed the time for herself. The agent was stunned, and so were we when we were told why our new executive secretary wouldn't be showing up for work. "What a waste," I thought. "What an awful waste."

Never did I imagine when I started the drug-testing program that I might actually be tossing a lifeline to someone.

Understand, I'm not judging the morality of recreational drug use here. I generally believe that what people do on their own time is their own business. Nor do I mean to suggest that every marijuana smoker or cocaine user is a thief, a safety risk, or a malingerer. Some people can, in fact, function under the influence of drugs. Our would-be executive secretary had glowing references.

I know, however, that someone who smokes crack at lunch or marijuana after hours is not able to give the company her or his best efforts at work, and that's what I ask of employees. I want them to do their best while we're paying them. In return, I'll do everything I can to make sure that their jobs are secure and that they have a good work environment.

A Life Turns Around

But there's another side to the drug-testing story that I didn't see until recently. The person who opened my eyes was Bruce Howard, the only employee who'd flunked the first drug test and passed the second. Since then, Bruce has advanced steadily in the company. He's now one of our top supervisors, with a whole department reporting to him. A few months ago, my wife, Elaine, and I took all eight of the supervisors out to lunch to thank them for their contributions. We handed out bonus checks and talked about the importance of their role and the difference they'd made at CitiStorage. Elaine then asked if anybody had anything to add.

Bruce stood up. He said, "I love it here, but I want to tell you I'm one of those who almost didn't make it." His first stint at the company hadn't lasted long. He'd been fired for absenteeism and poor performance. A few years later we hired him back, hoping he'd matured. Everything seemed to be going well until we started our drug-testing program and he failed the first test. "I came to a crossroads," Bruce said. "My job and my new life were important to me, but I realized I couldn't hold on to them unless I made a choice. Back then, I hung out with guys who smoked weed all the time. I knew that if I kept doing that, it would be too hard to quit. So I had to find new friends. I had to switch places I went to. I had to change all my routines. With the help of my fiancee, I did it. I changed my whole life. I became a more focused and serious person because, you know, you get rid of the distortion that comes from smoking weed. And I've never regretted making that choice. My life is better now in every way."

Never did I imagine when I started the drug-testing program that I might actually be tossing a lifeline to someone, but it sure makes me feel good to know I did.

2

Drug Testing in the Workplace Is Counterproductive

Barbara Ehrenreich

Barbara Ehrenreich is a columnist for the Progressive, *a magazine that focuses on such issues as First Amendment rights, racism, and the environment. As a writer who undertakes a diverse range of social and political issues, she is the author or coauthor of more than a dozen books, including* Fear of Falling: The Inner Life of the Middle Class *and* Nickel and Dimed: Surviving in Low-Wage America. *She has also written for a number of magazines, including* Ms., Harper's, *the* Nation, *the* New Republic, *the* Atlantic Monthly, *and the* New York Times Magazine.

An increasing number of employers are now testing job applicants and employees for illegal drug use despite evidence that indicates drug testing does not guarantee better performance. For example, studies show that drug testing does not reduce absenteeism and does not increase job safety. In addition, drug tests may be unreliable: They may provide a false-positive or false-negative result, and many drug users know how to thwart the test. Testing also can be extremely expensive, with little to show for it. Lastly, drug testing procedures compel current and potential employees to submit to humiliating circumstances. Unfortunately, the prevalence of drug testing by large companies has now inured Americans to these degrading and invasive procedures just so they may obtain and keep a job.

The fascination with urine remains undimmed through the ages. Until the arrival of scientific medicine, physicians subjected it to careful visual scrutiny, expecting the color and clarity to reveal an exact diagnosis. Today [in 2000], it's the corporate class that seems transfixed by the predictive powers of piss: 80 percent of large employers insist on testing job applicants' urine—or occasionally hair or blood—for damning traces of illegal substances. You can be the best qualified applicant in all other ways, but if your urine speaks against you, you're out. Experience, skill, enthusiasm, and energy— pee trumps them all.

An Irrational Concern

It's odd, given employers' lack of concern about the rest of their employees' private lives, that they take so much interest in the off-hour consumption of drugs. The members of the employing class, after all, don't seem to care whether their potential employees spend their weekends consuming kiddie porn or abusing their pets. Nor do most employers show the slightest concern about the adequacy of their employees' diets and housing arrangements. In fact, they will be delighted to hire you for $6 or $7 an hour even though, on wages like that, you will probably be unable to observe the most elementary proprieties, like living indoors and showering before showing up for work.

You can be the best qualified applicant in all other ways, but if your urine speaks against you, you're out.

Odder still, especially for those who think of capitalism as the most "rational" of economic systems, drug testing doesn't work, even on the employers' rather Scrooge-like terms. A report released [in] September [2000] by the ACLU [American Civil Liberties Union], "Drug Testing: A Bad Investment," summarizes studies showing that drug testing does not lower absenteeism, improve workplace safety, or achieve any of the other goals claimed for it by the anti-drug warriors. This should be no surprise: The tests mainly detect marijuana, which lingers in the body far longer than cocaine or heroin, and drug testing labs are often alarmingly inaccurate, in both the false-negative and false-positive directions. In addition, smart drug users have all kinds of ways of foiling the test, from the herb goldenseal (available in health food stores) to vials of drug-free, battery-warmed urine (available on the Web). More to the point, most drug users confine their drug using to their off hours, when it can have little or no possible effect on their job performance. The residual mental effects of a weekend joint, for example, are about as powerful as those of a Saturday night beer—i.e., nil. Not to mention the fact that one of the most disabling and addicting drugs, alcohol, isn't usually tested for at all.

And what exactly would it mean for drug testing to "work," anyway? An argument could be made for testing airline pilots and school bus drivers, on the grounds that an off-hour user might, just possibly, be tempted to take up while landing a 747 or driving on ice-coated streets. But retail and cleaning service workers? In my town, Winn-Dixie [a supermarket chain] tests applicants for a $6-an-hour job stacking Cheerio boxes; Howard Johnson tests applicants for bed-making jobs. Hudson News, which can be found in New York area airports, greets customers with a sign boasting that it's a "drug-free workplace," but is the newspaper you buy there any more interesting if the cashier is an abstainer rather than a stoner? An alcoholic rather than a coke head?

Speaking of newspapers, *The New York Times,* the *Los Angeles Times,* and *The Washington Post* all test their editors and writers—a practice that may actually make these papers less interesting, or at least help account for their unrelieved blandness. This is not because druggies make better reporters (though who knows?), but because any journalist sheep-like enough to submit to a urine test should, on this evidence alone, be barred from a profession that claims to value fearlessly independent thinking.

The High Cost of Drug Testing

In other areas, drug testing may actually be counterproductive. First, there's the cost. The ACLU reports that in 1990 the federal government spent $11.7 million to test 29,000 employees, only 153 of whom tested positive—amounting to a cost of $77,000 to detect each putative drug user! Then there's the likely effect of testing on morale. A 1998 study found that testing "reduced rather than enhanced productivity" by as much as 29 percent, apparently because it leads to a certain surliness among the workers.

Most drug users confine their drug using to their off hours, when it can have little or no possible effect on their job performance.

So why, in contempt of all the evidence, does American business remain so slavishly addicted to drug testing? Part of the answer has to be that drug testing is now a billion dollar industry, meaning that an awful lot of people have a stake in its health and longevity. Capitalism is supposed to operate in a briskly rational fashion, but profits can perpetuate any kind of foolishness. Hence, for example, the Congressional fondness for obsolete weapons systems: It doesn't matter if they can't fly or even if the Pentagon has adamantly rejected them; they keep [weapons manufacturers] Lockheed Martin and Boeing content.

Sheer herd mentality—"peer pressure," as it's known in the anti-drug movement—also contributes to the drug-testing habit. I once asked a hotel owner why he tests his employees, and he said, in so many words: Everyone else is doing it, and I don't want to be the one who gets stuck with all the druggies and lowlifes who can't get a job anywhere else in town. This sounded vaguely reasonable until he added that he couldn't, ha ha, pass one of those tests himself, which made me wonder: If one pot-head can make all the company's top decisions, why can't another one be trusted to push a broom?

A Humiliating Procedure

Nor can we eliminate the kinkier charms of drug testing—to the employer, that is. In some testing protocols, the hapless worker has to pull down her pants in front of a lab technician or attendant and then pee in the presence of that forbidding audience. This is not a medical procedure; it's a rite of humiliation, designed to send the employee the message: We own you, all of you, and our ownership extends way beyond 5 P.M. Similarly for those intrusive pre-employment "personality tests," with true-or-false propositions like "I often feel overwhelmed by self-pity." It's not really our urine that they want—or our blood or our hair—but our souls.

There are a few small, hopeful signs. Faced with a severe labor shortage, some Internet and computer firms are abandoning testing rather than drive away qualified applicants. In safety-sensitive industries, a few companies have taken up the far more pertinent practice of "performance testing"—gauging an employee's motor skills just prior to work.

But the damage to democracy has already been done. In a decade of testing, millions of Americans have grown inured to this invasion of their bodies and private lives, readily trading their Fourth Amendment protection from "unreasonable search" in exchange for a job. And submission, no less than drugs, can be a hard habit to break.

3

Workplace Drug Testing Is Cost Effective

Judith A. Swartley

Judith A. Swartley is the managing partner of M. Arthur Consulting Group, Inc., a firm located in Centreville, Delaware, that specializes in implementing substance abuse programs. She has written numerous articles and founded both the Women in Family Business Peer Group and the Lehigh Valley Safety Peer Group, an association of 120 companies that meets quarterly to discuss safety issues, problems, and concerns.

Without a drug testing program, companies are vulnerable to accidents that may cost the owners their business. The overall cost of workplace drug use is over $75 billion. A portion of that cost, statistics indicate, stems from a high percentage of worker's compensation claims that are drug-related and from the fact that employees with drug or alcohol problems are more likely to be injured. In one case, a company lost 20 percent of its workforce after implementing a drug testing policy; however, the company experienced only a small dip in revenue, and its employee morale increased. Of the three different types of workplace drug testing—pre-employment, post-accident, and random—random testing is the most effective in deterring drug use because employees never know if or when they will be tested. By implementing a random drug testing program, companies will experience *higher employee morale and productivity with lower insurance costs.*

"We can't afford to lose any employees in this tight labor market even if they are substance abusers." —vice president of $10 million construction company.

What this vice president didn't fully comprehend was that drug-users are only one-third as productive as nonabusers, three times [more] likely to be late, almost four times more likely to be in a workplace accident and five times more likely to file a workers' compensation claim, according to research from the National Institute on Drug Abuse.

And, what the owners of the company didn't realize was that their insurance would not pay a claim if it was drug-related and that shareholders could be personally liable for damages.

I recently consulted for a small company that suspected a few employees smoked marijuana. However, the concern became alarming when employees went into the office smelling like marijuana. This signaled several things: 1) the employees were smoking marijuana during working hours; 2) the employees were brazenly flaunting their habits because they knew the employer wouldn't do anything; and 3) the employees didn't realize the problems this would pose with customers and the company's reputation.

Drug-users are only one-third as productive as non-abusers, three times [more] likely to be late, almost four times more likely to be in a workplace accident.

More alarming, however, was the fact that the company could go out of business with one drug-related fatality lawsuit. In other words, the drug-user causing the accident would lose a job while the owners of the company would lose their business.

Different Types of Programs

In order to understand drug testing itself, let's step back and look at the different types of testing procedures:

- Pre-employment

- Post-accident

- Random

In general, pre-employment and post-accident drug testing are performed at most companies and serve to warn employees that the company is drug-free. However, most pre-employment and post-accident drug testing programs don't deter drug use. With pre-employment testing, users refrain from drugs during the job search so they can pass the test. Then, after accepting the new job, they often start using drugs again. Typically, if the person refrains from using drugs for three days or longer, they will pass a urine test.

Post-accident tests don't deter drug use because many small- to medium-sized companies forget to request a test after an accident or management can't determine when an accident is serious enough to require a test. As a result of their indecision, management simply doesn't test anyone.

Random tests, on the other hand, decrease and deter drug usage. One of the most critical elements of the program is its random nature—in both who is selected and how often the tests are performed. That is, you might decide to test 25 percent of your employees once a quarter.

Computer-based, random-name generated software keeps the process completely objective. Consequently, some employees might be tested several times in a row, or they may not be tested for a long period of time—the nature of random testing. It is for this reason, however that random testing both decreases and deters drug usage—employees don't know when they'll be tested. . . .

A Test Case

I've implemented substance abuse programs at companies that told me point blank that they didn't have a problem and I wouldn't find any "druggies" at their company. They made similar assertions that having a drug program would tell the employees that company management didn't trust them.

One such company that said it didn't have a problem decided to implement a random substance abuse program. They anticipated a mildly negative reaction to the announcement of the program, but the response was much more than mild. During the next week, employees stormed into the office one-by-one and told management this program was against their constitutional rights. Some even admitted smoking marijuana, but said it was on the weekends and that management had no right to control their free time.

The company held a voluntary evening meeting of all its employees, and let an attorney make a presentation and answer any questions. Management thought perhaps 50 percent of its employees would attend; however, they all attended. The employees patiently listened to the presentation, but afterward the questions came one after another with heated debate.

The company tried to be compassionate about the program and delayed the implementation by six months to allow employees to eliminate drugs from their systems. The company also offered free rehab with no repercussions to anyone who volunteered, and offered re-employment to any employee who completed a rehab program after testing positive.

After the first round of tests, the company had no positives. This confirmed the original impression. However, these results are exactly what to expect at the start. That is, the employees want to keep their jobs and will be careful for the first six months. After that, they typically start taking chances.

Results from Drug Testing

This is just what happened. In total, during the first year the company lost 20 percent of its workforce to marijuana and cocaine. Most of these people were the same ones who contested the program from the beginning. That was a staggering number, especially when it was compared to the national average of 10 percent.

However, the surprise was that sales did not decrease 20 percent with 20 percent fewer employees. Instead, sales attributed to the loss dipped 4 percent, thus fulfilling another prophecy—drug-users are only one-third as productive as drug-free employees.

The company didn't have any success stories regarding employees who entered rehab. Most dropped out during the process. In hindsight, the company should have eliminated the rehab provision from its policy. That is, if a person tests positive, he is now fired immediately. Although it seems compassionate to give an employee a chance, it also enables him to "take a chance" because he knows he won't be fired. Also, dealing with the rehab issue consumed far too much management time.

[Forty-seven] percent of all workers' compensation claims are related to substance abuse.

Strategically and financially, the company replaced the employees and has increased revenues. As an added benefit, it switched insurance carriers and saved approximately 20 percent of the premium partially due to the no-nonsense drug policy.

From a nonquantitative perspective, employees said they were glad the company implemented the program because they felt safer. Now they know the person working next to them is drug-free and probably won't contribute to an injury or death.

In turn, morale is higher. Not only do the employees feel safer, they know the company wouldn't tolerate drug-users.

Was it a headache? You bet. Would management do it again? Absolutely. The temporary dip in revenues was inconsequential to the increased morale among the employees, and it feels good to work in a drug-free environment.

Research on Drug Testing

Research usually convinces companies to proceed with random testing. Take your pick from the following:

- Only 3 percent of all companies with fewer than 200 employees have substance abuse programs, yet 47 percent or all workers' compensation claims are related to substance abuse, according to the Drugs in the Workplace Act.

- Employees diagnosed with drug or alcohol dependencies were up to 20 percent more likely to be injured on the job than those not abusing drugs or alcohol, according to the Pacific Institute.

- Only 3 percent of small businesses have drug testing programs and only 12 percent have a formal policy, according to the U.S. Department of Labor's Bureau of Labor Statistics. In contrast, among larger companies, those with 250 or more employees—46 percent test their workers and 74 percent have formal antidrug policies.

- Almost three-quarters of the nation's 11.7 million drug-users are employed and as many as 23 percent of them use illegal drugs on the job, according to the National Institute on Drug Abuse. The cost to businesses of drug use is $75 billion–$100 billion in lost productivity, higher health care costs and workers' compensation costs. Also, drug-users have higher absentee and tardiness rates than nonabusers.

4

Workplace Drug Testing Has Not Been Proven Cost Effective

Andy Meisler

Andy Meisler is a staff writer for Workforce Management, *a magazine that focuses on trends in human resource management. His articles include "Changes in Behavioral Benefits," "Think Globally, Act Rationally," and "A Matter of Degrees," the latter of which is about business tuition reimbursement.*

Attitudes toward workplace drug testing programs are changing primarily because more companies believe the benefits are outweighed by the costs. While proponents of drug testing cite anecdotal evidence that drug testing saves money because of greater employee productivity, lower turnover, and lower health care costs, there are no conclusive studies to prove this. For example, studies cited by drug testing proponents provide weak evidence, and others show that alcohol use has a greater impact on productivity than drug use. One study found that there was no difference in health care costs between those employees who smoke marijuana and those who do not. Another indicated that drug testing actually lowers productivity because talented applicants— those who can find work anywhere—are chased away, believing the company does not trust them or respect their privacy. Overall, research indicates that workplace drug testing programs do not pay off.

Joseph Reilly, a bearded middle-aged man who is the founder and president of Florida Drug Screening, Inc., stands at a lectern in a Washington, D.C., hotel meeting room less than 300 yards from the White House. His topic is selling employee drug-testing programs to small and medium-sized businesses. Reilly is preaching to the choir. He's speaking to 85 colleagues who are assembled at a daylong workshop organized by the Drug and Alcohol Testing Industry Association [DATIA].

The attendees are an earnest-looking group of primarily boomer-aged entrepreneurs and executives who seem utterly unconcerned about shifting attitudes toward their industry. As he speaks, members of the audience nod and scribble notes in "Drug and Alcohol Testing Programs for Non-Mandated Employers" workbooks.

What Reilly doesn't mention, and no one else in the room brings up, is this: the drug-testing industry is coming under scrutiny, its value questioned as never before. While the efficacy of drug testing continues to be a subject of debate, there is a more relevant question being raised at businesses where testing isn't a federally mandated safety requirement. Does workplace drug testing pay? While many in the field and their colleagues in government and industry speak optimistically of a time when every American worker, from the CEO on down, will have to prove his drug-free status, there's been a small but significant shift in corporate thinking. Under the pressure of hard times, neither the philosophical nor the economic reasons for drug testing are as convincing—or affordable—as they once were.

[In 2002] the American drug-testing industry conducted between 20 and 25 million tests and had revenues of $737 million, a growth of only 1 percent from the previous year. The drug-testing industry grew at an annual rate of 12.5 percent during the 1990s. However, [in 2001], according to the latest survey conducted by the American Management Association, 61 percent of companies administered drug tests to job applicants—down from 68 percent in 1996. In July [2003], Quest Diagnostics Inc., a leading processor of employee drug tests, which also provides diagnostic services to the medical industry, reported a 9 percent increase in revenue in the second quarter even though there was a 10 percent drop in the drug-testing portion of its business.

> *Neither the philosophical nor the economic reasons for drug testing are as convincing—or affordable—as they once were.*

Reduced hiring during the recession is responsible for much of the drop. But there are other causes. Meldron Young, the American Management Association's human resources practice consultant, says that a growing number of employers regard off-work-site marijuana use, which produces more than half of all positive results on non-mandated drug tests, as not worth the time, expense or hard feelings it costs to detect. "You have people moving into the upper echelons of corporate America now that kind of take the stance that if [casual off-site drug use] isn't affecting the person's performance, it's not an issue."

A Small, Quiet Revolt

The main theme of Reilly's speech is his own belief in the complete necessity, the absolute righteousness, of workplace drug testing. "Many of the fears and misconceptions surrounding drug testing have been resolved in the minds of employers," he declares. "The science of drug testing has passed the test of time."

That was not the conclusion of top executives at electronics giant Hewlett-Packard [in 2000], shortly before they decided to drop drug testing. So few applicants were testing positive, a company spokesperson said at the time, that the procedure was no longer cost effective. Cisco and Sun Micro-systems, like many other high-tech firms that attract highly skilled, self-motivated employees, have never conducted drug tests.

Neither does Trader Joe's, a 200-store nationwide specialty supermarket chain. Carol Impara, vice president for human resources, says that the company doesn't test because of the value it places on creating employee trust. "Basically, it's want-ing to show that we trust people, and showing that from the start," she says. "Our managers aren't sitting in their offices, they're out there with everybody else. It's a team effort."

On the other hand, a number of firms whose CEOs or workforce executives were recommended by DATIA members as proud, satisfied consumers of their drug-testing services, in-cluding Sheetz, a fast-growing chain of convenience stores, and Carrier West, a heating and air conditioning distribution company in Denver, either refuse to comment or don't re-spond to telephone calls. Other firms that will comment offer statements that are less than illuminating. Hewlett-Packard, for instance, has backed off its two-year-old financial explana-tion for suspending drug testing and now cites its company-wide code of conduct, summarized by the phrase "HP must maintain the highest standards of integrity," as the reason it no longer tests for drug use. Its arch rival Dell Inc. cites the exact same reason for taking the opposite approach. It tests every one of its approximately 42,000 employees.

The Bottom Line

One significant reason for this inconsistency is that no com-panies that administer such tests have conducted any studies of either the efficacy or effect of their own drug-testing pro-grams on the bottom line. Beverly Potter, a consultant on cor-porate drug testing and co-author of both *Drug Testing at Work: A Guide for Employers* and *Pass the Test: An Employee*

Guide to Drug Testing, says that to do so would be at best irrelevant and at worst embarrassing. "They're worried about their image," Potter says. "They're afraid that to say they don't support drug testing implies that they support drug use."

She and other critics of drug testing charge private, industry drug testers with capitalizing on such corporate caution. They rely on vague ROI [return on investment] figures extrapolated from decades-old research studies. The by-no-means undisputed results of these studies are used to show the undeniable financial incentives of screening for the presence of marijuana, cocaine, heroin, PCP, amphetamines and up to a dozen or more other illicit substances in employees' bodies. The benefits are said to include increased productivity, fewer accidents, lower health-care costs and decreased employee turnover. The next rhetorical bulwark is the Drug-Free Workplace Act of 1988, which requires companies doing $25,000 or more in business with the federal government per year to certify that they are, well, a drug-free workplace. The act does not, however, require a drug-testing program.

No companies that administer such tests have conducted any studies of either the efficacy or effect of their own drug-testing programs on the bottom line.

Additional arguments for drug testing include the absolute necessity of preventing drug-induced workplace accidents. It is also argued that drug testing can work as a kind of informal IQ test to screen out job applicants too dim to abstain before a pre-announced drug test, and that the average employee is revolted by the prospect of working alongside unsafe or work-shirking individuals who are under the influence of drugs. Professional drug testers also introduce the possibility of armies of drug-addicted job applicants showing up at the front door of employers that don't do drug tests alter being turned away by drug-testing employers.

Given a cost of only $25 to $35 per urine test per employee, down to $14 to $28 for companies of more than about 10,000 employees, these talking points were surefire deal clinchers during boom times. Moreover, in an era when DARE [Drug Abuse Resistance Education] chapters are in most school districts despite evidence that they do little to prevent student drug abuse, and an anti-drug-testing position can be easily twisted by politicians or competitors into a "pro-drug" stance, most companies are loath to even mention the matter of drug testing. But with a stagnating economy, the pro-testing arguments are not the slam-dunks they once were.

The American Management Association's Meldron Young says that many companies that previously demanded drug tests of both job applicants and current employees are now testing only job applicants. Lewis Maitby, president of the liberal National Workrights Institute in Princeton, New Jersey, points out that the economic climate has significantly changed corporate attitudes about drug testing. "Initially, in the late '80s or early '90s, employers looked at drug testing and said, 'Why not?'" Maitby says. "Now employers look at drug testing like everything else and say, 'Where's the payoff?' And if nobody sees a payoff, programs get cut—or, more often, cut back."

The Case Against Drug Testing

The meatiest part of Reilly's presentation is his own tried-and-true sales pitch, which he illustrates with the aid of a felt-tip pen and a whiteboard. Since 17 percent of the American population are currently substance abusers, he says, and since substance-abusing employees cost their businesses a national average of $7,000 a piece per year, the ROI yielded by yearly drug tests is a stunning 288 percent. Additionally, companies that use drug testing enjoy reduced absenteeism and turnover, increased productivity and fewer accidents.

What he doesn't mention is the considerable body of research that supports the economic case against drug testing. Much of this research was conducted by respected academicians and government agencies. The most convenient access to this information, however, is through two unabashedly political organizations: the National Organization for the Reform of Marijuana Laws [NORML] and the American Civil Liberties Union [ACLU].

On NORML's Web site, nestled among advertisements for polo shirts made of hemp-based cloth and appeals against police harassment of "rave" parties, is a reference to a 1990 article in *Scientific American* by John Horgan, one of that publication's senior writers at the time. He explores the genesis of a finding by the federal government's National Institute on Drug Abuse [NIDA] that illegal drug use costs American society $47 billion, in 1990 dollars, per year.

Many companies that previously demanded drug tests of both job applicants and current employees are now testing only job applicants.

"Here's how the figure was derived," Horgan writes. "In 1982 NIDA surveyed 3,700 households around the country. The Research Triangle Institute [RTI], a NIDA contractor in North Carolina, then analyzed the data and found that the household income of adults who had ever smoked marijuana daily for a month, or at least 20 out of 30 days, was 28 percent less than the income of those who hadn't. The RTI analysts called this difference 'reduced productivity due to daily marijuana use.' They calculated the total 'loss,' when extrapolated to the general population, at $26 billion. Adding the estimated costs of drug-related crimes, accidents and medical care produced a grand total of $47 billion for 'costs to society of drug abuse.'"

In Horgan's opinion this conclusion is scientifically inde-
fensible. Marijuana-reform activists and representatives of
other civil-libertarian organizations chime in that urine tests,
which register positive for marijuana use if the test subject has
used the drug even once in the previous one to three months,
are the wrong instruments for filtering out hard-core users
anyway.

Research on Drug Testing

Other anti-drug-testing arguments are available from the
ACLU, which in 1999 issued a little-noticed 28-page report
titled *Drug Testing: A Bad Investment.* This report criticizes the
methodology and conclusions of studies frequently cited by
members of the drug testing industry. It confirms the
workforce-wide substance-abuse figure of 17 percent—but
adds that the substance most often abused is alcohol.

Most claims of reduced absenteeism, turnover and inju-
ries, it contends, are based on several late-1980s studies of
postal and power workers, which the ACLU interprets quite
differently. The organization says that the studies are either in-
conclusive or show no correlation between drug use and poor
or dangerous workplace performance. The ACLU concedes
that one postal study does show a correlation between drug
use and turnover/termination. It also points out that the same
data shows an equally strong correlation, unmentioned by the
pro-drug testers, between the likelihood of a new postal worker
quitting or being fired and simply being African-American.

The ACLU report also quotes a much longer but no less
obscure study, "Under the influence? Drugs and the American
Work Force," also commissioned by NIDA. Among that 1994
study's conclusions, the ACLU points out, were that the data
"[does] not provide clear evidence of the deleterious effects of
drugs other than alcohol on safety and other job-performance
indicators" and that "widely cited cost estimates of the effects
of alcohol and other drug use on U.S. productivity are based

on questionable assumptions and weak measures." The ACLU report also includes a Kaiser Permanente study that compared the medical histories and health-care costs of people who used marijuana and those who did not. Kaiser found no significant differences. Theoretically at least, that means that pot-smokers don't strain their employers' health-plan budgets any more than their abstinent cohorts.

Much of the data on drug testing is inconveniently and annoyingly contrary to the conventional wisdom and cannot be ignored.

The ACLU cites an $11.7 million drug-testing program, conducted in 1990, that uncovered 153 drug users out of 29,000 government employees tested. The organization calculates that it cost taxpayers $77,000 for each drug abuser found by the program. Then, as its pièce de résistance, the ACLU points to yet another study, this one commissioned by a pro-labor publication, *Working USA,* and carried out by economists from Le Moyne College, a small Jesuit-run school in Syracuse, New York. The 1998 report, it says, proves that drug testing can actually decrease productivity. It allegedly does this by dissuading talented high-tech workers, who have a choice of employers, from working for companies that they feel do not trust them or respect their privacy. This limits the already small and select hiring pool for these companies.

Drug-Testing Industry Response

The drug-testing industry generally treats these reports with scorn. It advises doubters, in effect, to value the drug testers' experiences on the front lines above dry, abstract studies and, above all, to consider just who is making the arguments against them. Susan Ramsden, a forensic toxicologist who is founder and president of Comprehensive Medical Center, a drug-testing service in Sacramento, California, says that whatever the national statistics happen to show, she does business in what she believes to be the illegal amphetamine production and consumption capital of the world, parts of Northern California.

"If I go into warehouses, small construction companies or temp agencies that use day labor, we'll have as high as a 30 percent positive drug rate," Ramsden says. "When I get a call from a business owner, saying, 'Oh my God, I just was told we have a problem,' or 'I've just found some drugs,' I've sometimes found 100 percent of his employees positive for amphetamines."

Eric Hess, a DATIA board member and vice president of drug and alcohol testing services for U.S. Investigations Services in Annandale, Pennsylvania, scans the 1999 ACLU report and says, "This was written around the time in which the ACLU was trying to fortify a position that states should legalize marijuana use." He mentions the increased abuse of amphetamines and "designer drugs" like Ecstasy in recent years, and declares that the ACLU policy is badly out of date. Referring to the organization's stance, he adds, "This is obviously a political commentary."

A History of Workplace Drug Testing

The modern history of workplace drug testing began in 1986, when President Ronald Reagan signed an executive order declaring all federal agencies drug-free workplaces. In 1991 President George Bush the elder signed the Omnibus Transportation Employee Testing Act, which, among other measures, mandated pre-employment and post-accident drug and alcohol testing for safety-sensitive workers such as truck drivers, airline pilots, and maritime, pipeline and railway workers. Unannounced random drug tests for 50 percent of all safety-sensitive workers per year were mandated. Over the years, as the percentage of positive tests has stabilized at about 2 percent, the random-testing requirement has been progressively lowered to 25 percent for several industries, including airlines and railroads.

Private industry initially adopted non-mandated testing programs enthusiastically. Although civil libertarians and marijuana advocates quickly took employers like Southern Pacific and Times Mirror Co. to court, accusing them of invading their privacy or conducting illegal searches, a number of cases established the right of private employers, under the "at will" employment principle, to mandate pre-employment drug tests. To a lesser extent, other cases gave employers the right to institute tests on current employees on the grounds of reasonable suspicion. Nancy Delogu, a partner in the Washington, D.C., office of Littler Mendelson, a large labor and employment law firm, says the playing field has been tilted toward employers since the early 1990s. "We haven't seen a new restriction on [workplace] drug testing in years," she says. William Rittenberg, a lawyer in New Orleans who is a member of NORML's legal committee, is also familiar with the situation and agrees that employers have the upper hand. "I get calls from fired private-sector workers all the time," he says. They tell him they've tested positive. "I tell them, 'I'm sorry. I'm afraid you're out of luck.'"

This may not be the case for much longer. When the economy picks up, say experts brave enough to tackle the uncomfortable subject, employers facing a sellers' market will have to put aside their feelings and assumptions and address the subject of drug testing anew. Companies certainly will be against employee drug use, but they'll make their point about their disapproval of drugs without testing bodily fluids, says Roger Herman, a management consultant and head of The Herman Group in Greensboro, North Carolina. "They'll have to be more open, more tolerant."

Like the supposed economic benefits that brand-new publicly funded NFL stadiums bring to their local economies, or

the effectiveness of "boot camps" in turning teenage delinquents into productive citizens, the absolute necessity of employee drug testing now has the status of a concept that, well,
just feels right, conclude many of those close to the issue. For
complicated and mostly admirable reasons, few companies are
inclined to question these good feelings too deeply. But much
of the data on drug testing is inconveniently and annoyingly
contrary to the conventional wisdom and cannot be ignored.

5

Drug Tests Are Unreliable

Dana Hawkins

Dana Hawkins is a contributing editor with U.S. News & World
Report. *Hawkins's articles include "The Dark Side of Genetic
Testing" and "A Healthy Dose of Privacy," the latter of which is
about protecting patients' medical records.*

*Although drug test companies assert the complete accuracy of
their tests, some critics are questioning the tests' reliability. For
example, people who do not use illegal drugs can test positive for
drugs because the tests mistake medicine, food, or air-borne con-
taminates for traces of illegal substances. Studies show that the
least expensive drug tests, favored by employers, are also the
most error-prone. The accuracy of some on-site urine tests can be
as low as 52 percent. Even the laboratory urine test used for federal employees sometimes provides incorrect results. Sweat patch
and hair tests are fallible as well because of exposure to outside
particulates. Despite the risk of inaccurate results, most organizations do not retest because it is costly. As a consequence,
peoples' lives can be ruined because of faulty drug tests.*

D rug tests don't lie, people do. That's what Michelle Dunson used to think back when she administered urine tests
for a temp agency near Toledo, Ohio. Sometimes when she
told applicants they'd failed, the response would be wide-eyed
silence, then tears and denial. She offered them tissue, but
little sympathy.

Dunson later took a job with Whirlpool, where she was
injured [in 2000]. When she returned, she tested positive for
an opiate and was fired—even though a note from her doctor

outlined her prescriptions for a nonnarcotic painkiller, which she believes threw off the test. She has a wrongful-termination suit pending against Whirlpool, which stands by its testing. "I feel tremendous guilt now when I think of those who came to me nearly hysterical, saying they did not do drugs," says Dunson. "I think: My God, at least a few of them were probably telling the truth."

Dunson can be forgiven for believing drug test results were the gospel truth. The tests are often heralded as infallible, and many private and government employers, along with school principals and judges, put their faith in them. Half of major U.S. firms now test their employees, and more than 500 school districts have screening programs. But reliably picking up drug traces that linger days after a user's last high, while ignoring contaminants and similar-looking compounds in medicine and food, is a tall order for even the best technology. In the real world, technical glitches can mean mistakes— so-called false positives.

The fastest-growing segment of the drug-testing industry consists of newer and often more error-prone tests.

For employers who test to deter drug use, which they say leads to a safer, more productive workplace, so-so accuracy might be enough. But it comes at a high cost in reputations and livelihoods for those falsely accused. "Innocent people are being mislabeled because of unreliable products designed to cast a wide net," says Steven Karch, a medical researcher and author of *Karch's Pathology of Drug Abuse.*

Rising Error Rates

The error rates are likely to rise. While the traditional method—lab-based urine testing—can be highly reliable when done carefully, the fastest-growing segment of the drug-testing industry consists of newer and often more error-prone tests. On-site urine testing appeals to private employers because it gives results in minutes and can cost as little as $3 per screening. Yet studies of the cheapest of these tests, designed to pick up a single drug type such as amphetamines, show they give the right answer as little as one third of the time. Other new tests, which rely on lab analysis of hair and sweat, can be a powerful probe of drug use—but can also be fooled by stray drug molecules from the environment. . . .

Currently, laboratory urine testing—the "gold standard" test—is the only type allowed for federal employees. Samples are probed with antibodies for THC (marijuana), cocaine, opiates, PCP, and amphetamines, and checked to be sure they aren't doctored or too dilute. When a worker tests positive, the federal program mandates a second, more accurate confirmation test called gas chromatography-mass spectrometry, GC-MS, along with an interview with a medical review officer to be sure that another substance isn't causing a false positive. The sample's chain of custody is carefully documented as well.

Even GC-MS is not perfect, however. The test works by extracting and heating molecules from a sample and using an electric field to separate and identify them. Kent Holtorf, a physician and expert on drug-testing accuracy, says he got 1,500 calls [in 2001] from people asking for help with what they said were lab errors. He says that when a lab uses GC-MS to identify the entire range of molecules, it is 95 percent to 99 percent accurate. But Holtorf says labs don't always use the equipment to its full advantage. "Accuracy rates are going down, not up, as employers contract with the lowest-bidding lab," he says. It's cheaper to use GC-MS to look only for a few fragments of the drug molecules, which raises the risk of mistaking legitimate medicines, herbs, and foods like poppy seeds for illegal drugs.

No Second Chance

The drug-testing industry dismisses these concerns. "People

always come up with cockamamie stories about how their test result is wrong," says Paul Rust, a vice president at Quest Diagnostics. "But the GC-MS process is 100 percent accurate." Not quite, says Michael Martin, who is HIV-positive and takes the prescription drug Sustiva. The Worcester, Mass., resident says he had to take a pre-employment urine test after he was offered a job at Sears. He presented a doctor's letter saying his medication could cause him to test positive for pot. When just that happened, Sears rescinded the offer. "I want to work so badly I can taste it," says Martin. "But I can't stop taking my prescription just to test clean."

Sears, which is investigating Martin's case, says its policy is to confirm positive results with a second test. But at many companies, employees who fail the initial screen get no second chance. "Most employers, even those who use a lab, don't confirm positives on pre-employment tests," says David Evans, director of the National On-Site Testing Association. "It wouldn't be a financially smart thing to do." And, in most cases, it's perfectly legal not to. There are no regulations, other than a smattering of state laws, regarding testing of nongovernment workers.

Accuracy rates are going down, not up, as employers contract with the lowest-bidding lab.

Nor has there been tough scrutiny of the newer drug-testing technologies. "The lack of scientific studies on these devices is most surprising," says Amanda Jenkins, coauthor of the new book *On-Site Drug Testing*. The U.S. Food and Drug Administration will approve a test based solely on a company's own studies. Still, drug-testing veterans, some independent studies, and even the makers' own data suggest that three leading "alternative technologies" can be disturbingly error prone.

Three Alternative Tests

On-site testing. Like lab assays, these tests work by combining urine with antibodies. If the test is negative, a line appears on a test strip. But seeing the lines can be a judgment call, and some products are especially hard to read. "We stopped using a few tests because some people would see a line where others wouldn't," says Brian Walters of Premier Drug Testing in Russell Springs, Ky. In one study, 17 common on-site tests were used to analyze specimens; most contained either no drugs or trace amounts. The accuracy ranged from 52 percent to 82 percent.

Sweat patch. In this test, a Band-Aid-like patch attached to the skin collects sweat for up to seven days and is later lab-tested for drug residue. It's tough to cheat—if the patch is removed, it can't be reattached—and the test is often used in parole, probation, and child-custody cases to determine whether a user has been rehabilitated. But studies by the U.S. Naval Research Lab and the patch manufacturer itself showed that drug molecules from outside sources—such as clothes or other people—can penetrate the patch and trigger a false positive. The sole maker, PharmChem, says both studies exposed the patch to unrealistically high levels of contamination. "Those were just not real-world situations," says Neil Fortner, PharmChem's chief scientific officer. But a federal court in New York recently ruled that the sweat patch "is susceptible to outside contamination."

Sheryl Woodhall thinks that's what cost her custody of her two youngest children. She wore the patches to prove she was no longer a methamphetamine addict. But after she flunked seven of eight tests, her kids were placed permanently in foster care, and she was forbidden to contact them. During the same period, Woodhall says she tested negative on dozens of urine screens, done under observation so she couldn't cheat.

Hair tests. Lab analysis of 1.5-inch long strands of hair cut near the scalp can give a drug history covering 90 days, compared with only a few days for most drugs in urine tests. Psychemedics, the largest hair tester, says 140 schools and 2,300 corporate clients use its services. But hair testing is also the most controversial of the new technologies because of concerns that it is discriminatory and can be thrown off by contaminants. Several studies by the National Institute on Drug Abuse show that some drug molecules, whether ingested or picked up from the environment, have an affinity for the pigment melanin and bind more strongly to dark hair than light. "If two employees use cocaine, the blond might barely test negative, and the other will get caught," says Robert Stephenson of the Substance Abuse and Mental Health Services Administration.

Raymond Kubacki, president of Psychemedics, dismisses concerns about discrimination and says a series of washes removes contaminants from hair samples. "You could be in a crack den and you won't test positive." But Ronnie Jones, a Boston police officer for 20 years, blames contamination for a marginally positive result for cocaine he got on a hair test [in] March [2002]. Jones—nicknamed "the deacon" for his Bible reading and clean living—submitted a second hair sample the same day, which tested negative. Although the company downplays the contamination risk, Kubacki says it has begun testing for drug metabolites, the fingerprints left after drugs are processed by the body, rather than just the parent substances.

So far there have been few technical challenges to another new test, which relies on analysis of a saliva sample. Because drugs show up in saliva more quickly than in urine, hair, and sweat, the test may reveal whether a person is currently high, making it useful for post-accident testing. But it is just beginning to catch on. And like the other tests, it will get its real trial in the real world, where jobs and reputations will hinge on the right answer.

6

Student Drug Testing Is Beneficial

Calvina L. Fay

Calvina L. Fay is the executive director of Drug Free America Foundation, Inc. and former executive director of Houston's Drug-Free Business Initiative. She is also cofounder of Save Our Society, an antidrug legislation lobbying group that fights medical marijuana and regulation initiatives.

Drug testing effectively identifies and prevents drug use. In the academic realm, it helps to ensure that those students participating in athletics and extracurricular activities are drug free and able to focus on schoolwork. While some critics may say drug testing is inaccurate, new procedures remove the possibility of false results: tracking specimens closely, administering confirmation tests, and requiring physician follow-up. Coupled with education programs, drug testing is an effective deterrent against drug use and should be implemented for all students before a tragedy occurs.

In his 2004 State of the Union address, President [George W.] Bush not only endorsed student drug testing, but he asked for $23 million in additional government funds to implement such programs nationwide. For those in the drug abuse prevention field, this decision was paradigmatic, a firm description of what should be. Although some feel student

Calvina L. Fay, "Student Drug Testing Is Part of the Solution: When Combined with Effective Drug Education, It Prevents Tragedy," *Behavioral Health Management,* July/ August 2004. Copyright © 2004 by Medquest Communications, LLC. Reproduced by permission.

drug testing is invasive, there is no denying it is an effective tool for identifying and preventing drug problems.

The intent of such programs is not to punish students. The goals are to deter drug use and for the drug user to straighten out his or her life. The results are not turned over to law enforcement; rather, they are discussed with the parents of the child in question so, as a family, they can discuss which type of drug treatment is suitable for their child. Drug use affects cognitive abilities and attention span, making it difficult for the user to properly learn and succeed in school. The benefits of student drug testing in addressing this abound.

The goals [of drug testing] are to deter drug use and for the drug user to straighten out his or her life.

School drug testing, as implemented today [in 2004], applies only to students who voluntarily choose to participate in athletic and extracurricular activities. Student athletes and students in extracurricular activities take leadership roles in the school community and, as role models, should be drug-free—and student drug testing helps ensure this. More importantly, it gives students in extracurricular activities an "out" or an argument that they can use with drug-using peers when pressured to take drugs (e.g., "If I take drugs, the coach will know because I have to take a drug test, and then I'll be kicked off the team"). Today, drug testing is a standard procedure when applying for a job. Certainly, athletes who want to compete at the collegiate or Olympic level should get used to the idea of drug testing.

Misconceptions About Drug Testing

Some people criticize drug testing on grounds it can be inaccurate. This charge is incorrect. The drug-testing procedures in place [in 2004] eliminate the possibility of a false positive. If schools follow drug-testing procedures recommended by the White House Office of National Drug Control Policy, students will provide a urine specimen in a private rest-room area. The specimen will be handled under the chain of custody guidelines, a set of procedures to account for the integrity of each urine specimen by tracking its handling and storage from collection to disposition of the specimen. If the screening test is positive, confirmation is sought with a more sensitive test. If the confirmation test is positive, a physician trained in drug testing then reviews it and contacts the student to see if there is a legitimate medical reason for the positive result. Drug test results are confidential, and federal law prevents them from being released outside the school. And the results do not follow the student once he or she leaves high school (as per the Family Educational Rights and Privacy Act).

Another misconception about student drug testing is that it is expensive and difficult to implement. A drug test costs only between $10 and $30 per student, a cost that is nominal compared to its true worth. Any school that receives federal education funding is permitted to use these funds for drug testing; the No Child Left Behind Act specifically authorizes the expenditure of federal education funds for student drug testing. So, if the money is there, let's put it to good use.

Education and Testing Work Together

I have worked with many like-minded individuals on this issue who all agree that student drug testing is a deterrent, although effective only when coupled with other drug-prevention and -education initiatives. Along these lines, attorney David Evans is making many important strides with the Drug-Free Schools Coalition in New Jersey. Evans stresses an important point when he says, "Many schools find great value in using random drug and alcohol testing [for student athletes and those in extracurricular activities] as part of their antidrug programs. The goal of drug testing is to deter drug and alcohol use. Students who know they may be detected are less likely to use drugs or alcohol, not to mention experience the consequences of addiction."

The unfortunate part of student drug testing today is that we cannot test those who do not participate in extracurricular activities. These students encounter the same peer pressure that the extracurricular students face, but they don't have the same drug-testing defense, making it potentially more difficult to say no to drugs. Although schools that test athletes and students in other extracurricular activities experience an overall decline in drug use, they must not forget about those students who do not benefit from drug testing and at least provide them with other drug-prevention and -education alternatives.

As a drug-policy and -prevention expert with more than 20 years' experience, I have fought for this issue alongside many parents who have lost their children to drugs. These parents have told me time and time again, "I never suspected that my child was using drugs. If I had only known, I could have done something." It kills me every time I hear this. Student drug testing is one of the best ways to identify a problem and offer a chance for parents to know about it and get help before it is too late.

7

Student Drug Testing Alienates Students from Schools

Laura L. Finley and Peter S. Finley
Laura L. Finley is a former high school social studies teacher.
She holds a PhD in sociology from Western Michigan University
and has published articles on crime and race in the media. Her
research interests include student privacy rights, in particular is-
sues regarding drug testing of student athletes. Peter S. Finley is
a former high school teacher and coach. He is now a doctoral
student in Sport Administration at the University of Northern
Colorado and works with the Sport Marketing Research Insti-
tute. He has researched sociology of sport issues such as the de-
piction of student athletes in popular culture.

Drug testing does not work as a deterrent to student drug use.
Studies indicate no difference in student drug use between schools
that utilize drug tests and those that do not. Another study
found drug testing fostered more positive attitudes toward drug
use among students. Not only can it cultivate unsafe attitudes,
drug testing may provoke unforeseen consequences: Students are
forced to reveal personal medical information to avoid false out-
comes on their tests, while some families are ostracized by their
community because they refuse to submit their child to a drug
test. Drug testing also conveys the idea that students should not
expect privacy. These consequences serve to alienate students

from what is supposed to be an enriching academic environment.

> Should we believe the self-serving, ever-growing drug
> enforcement/drug treatment bureaucrats, whose pay and
> advancement depends on finding more and more people to
> arrest and 'treat'? More Americans die in just one day in
> prisons, penitentiaries, jails and stockades than have ever
> died from marijuana throughout history. Who are they pro-
> tecting? From what?
>
> —*Dr. Fred Oerther*

Right off the bat let us assure the reader of one thing: Drug
testing doesn't work. It never has and likely never will. Do
drug tests sometimes catch people? Sure. But does it change
behavior as intended? Absolutely not, and if behavior does
change it is typically only for the worse as drug users pursue
new drugs that will escape detection. Drug testing is a first
strike in what quickly becomes an arms race between the
testers and those interested in beating the test, with the cheats
almost invariably staying a step ahead. This is true even when
the testers are armed with the most recent and extravagant
technology and extremely deep pockets. Schools are armed
with neither. . . .

Who Is Testing and How

Estimates of the percentage of schools with drug testing policies vary. Most studies place it at approximately 18–20%. According to a [2004] study by the University of Michigan Institute for Social Research, the group of students most commonly
tested are those "for cause," or based on some suspicion. Four-
teen percent of the reporting schools reported testing for
cause. Athletes are the next group most frequently tested, followed by students who volunteer for testing and students who
are on school probation. Approximately two percent of the re-
sponding schools test students involved in extracurriculars be-
sides athletics. Most testing programs are instituted in high

schools, although some middle schools have them as well. While only 200 schools currently randomly test their entire student body, Drug Czar John Walters [head of the office of National Drug Control Policy] is on tour stumping for greater use as we write this. . . .

The Pro-Testing Position

The primary reason cited for drug testing has shifted from the protection argument to deterrence. Drug Czar John Walters has proclaimed, "As a deterrent, few methods work better or deliver clearer results." Likewise, former New Orleans District Attorney Harry Connick has gone on the record stating, "There is one method that stands out as the most effective prevention method today, and that is student drug testing. (It is) the most effective demand-reduction tool, I believe, that this country has ever known. . . ." President Bush has even pledged $24 million to drug testing. In the slippery-slope argument so often made by the drug warriors and anti-teen conservatives, Walters asserts that, if we do not drug test our students, we are failing to protect them from drug use and addiction. So if we don't test we must be doing nothing? Worse, we're supporting teen drug use? Not surprising, given the source, the claim that schools can either test students or fail to protect them reeks of being short-sighted political rhetoric intended to label any who oppose the new drug testing culture.

Drug Testing Is Not a Deterrent

Like drug testing in professional sports and the workplace, drug testing of students has not proven effective. Most studies to date have addressed the efficacy of drug testing athletes, as testing policies for students involved in other activities are relatively new and thus have yet to be evaluated thoroughly. Results of the largest-scale national study on school drug testing, released in May of 2003, show that screenings in school do not discourage kids from using drugs. Simply put: The deterrence argument is bunk. The study, which involved 76,000 students nationwide and spanned several years, found drug use to be just as prevalent in schools with testing as in those without. According to the study, 37 percent of 12th grade students in schools with testing had smoked marijuana in the previous year, compared with 36 percent in schools without testing. Similar results were found for every grade level and for every illegal substance considered. The study measured prevalence, or percent reporting any use in the last 12 months, and frequency of use in the last year. Additional analyses addressed specific sub-groups of students. It was found that use of any illicit substances by male athletes was not significantly different in schools that tested compared to those that did not. The investigation even looked specifically at self-reported marijuana users (defined as those students who reported smoking more than twenty times in their lifetime) to assess whether drug testing would decrease numbers of heavy users. Results again did not differ significantly, indicating there was the same percentage of serious pot smokers in schools whether they test or not. The study also addressed whether policies allowing random testing of the entire student body were any more effective than not testing at all. While only seven of the 891 schools surveyed reported having such a policy, no statistically significant differences were found between these schools and those that do not test their student body.

> *Do drug tests sometimes catch people? Sure. But does it change behavior as intended? Absolutely not.*

Proponents of drug testing suggest the rate of usage possibly would have been even higher had the districts not imposed drug testing. Yet the researchers feel this is extremely unlikely, as they controlled for behavioral factors typically associated with substance abuse, including truancy. One of the researchers, Dr. Lloyd D. Johnston, said, "It's the kind of intervention that doesn't win the hearts and minds of children. I don't think it brings about any constructive changes in their attitudes about drugs or their belief in the dangers associated with using them."

Another study found that athletes in schools with drug testing programs reported more negative attitudes toward testing and more positive attitudes about drugs. When compared to students from schools without drug testing, the tested students were less likely to believe that there are negative consequences of drug use and more likely to believe that there are benefits of drug use. They believed their peers used more drugs, and believed their peers and authority figures were more tolerant of drug use. They also held less positive attitudes toward drug testing, less belief in its efficacy, and less belief in its potential benefits. Finally, the athletes in schools with drug testing reported less fear of the consequences of testing positive. So, not only does testing fail to decrease drug use but it also seems to foster dangerous attitudes about drugs amongst the tested population. University of Michigan researcher Johnston admitted that, "one could imagine situations where drug testing could be effective, if you impose it in a sufficiently draconian manner . . . that is, testing most kids and doing it frequently." However, the researchers, as well as the authors, do not advocate such a measure. . . .

Unconsidered Costs

As with drug testing in the workplace, there are several concerns with school drug testing that often go unconsidered. One is that students are forced to reveal any physical or emotional difficulties they may be having that require them to take medication. The point in requiring this admission is that the metabolites produced by some legal medications are identical to those of illegal drugs, so testers must be made aware in advance so as not to falsely accuse a student. Yet, since most students being tested are completely unaware of which substances could be misinterpreted, they have no choice but to list everything they take. One student objected to the requirement to list the prescription drugs she takes, but eventually submitted because she wanted to participate in extracurriculars in order to get into a good college.

The deterrence argument is bunk.

In addition to the fact that students must disclose personal information, the privacy of the test results remains in question. . . . While most policies of late mandate that urinalysis results are only provided to appropriate school officials, the student, and his or her parent or guardian, there are instances where results are given to police. Further, exactly what measures schools take to ensure that no other students or unnecessary faculty members will see the results is unclear. While it's bad enough that your school principal knows you're taking Prozac, it would be much worse if the student body or faculty became aware of your prescription against your will. The confidentiality problem is only likely to worsen. Addressing complaints about the immodest testing conditions being used by Olentangy Middle School in Ohio, the coordinator of the district's program, Joseph Franz, explains that, judging by the success of his company Sport Safe Testing Services, new schools will be constructed with built-in testing facilities. Well, it seems that chemistry class experiments are going to get a whole new twist but we have to wonder, do prisons even have their own drug testing facilities?

The treatment of people who object to drug testing is yet another concern. The Tannahills[1] objected to a mandatory drug test for their son, who was being targeted for testing along with his entire sixth grade class. They received threats from the community for their stance. Parents were told if they refused to sign the form allowing their child to be tested, it

---

1. In the Tannahills' case against Lockney Independent School District, the court would not permit random drug testing of all students.

would be presumed that he or she was using drugs. In this case, students would be punished with in-school suspension and banned temporarily from participation in extra-curricular activities. One of the nicer community members simply berated the Tannahills' parenting: "If either one of my children were doing drugs, I'd want them to get help. I don't see what the big deal is," said Pat Garza. Others reacted even less maturely to the Tannahills' exercising their right to object; someone shot their dog with a paintball and a note was left on their door saying, "You're messing with our kids." Letters to the editor published in the local paper suggested that the family move. Mighty neighborly behavior with some frightening implications. It's no longer just school administrators pushing these tests in violation of constitutional rights—it's other parents. This should ring an alarm bell for anyone concerned with civil liberties.

Increasing Student Disdain for School

Barring kids who test positive, or, even worse, those who are constitutionally-aware and refuse to consent to a drug test, from participation in extracurricular activities simply serves to increase students' disdain for school and prevents them from benefiting from all the positives associated with participation. In addition to the fact that participation in something additional to the regular school day is virtually required for college admittance, activities like the Debate Club and National Honor Society can build citizenship skills. According to Richard Glen Boire, counsel for the Center for Cognitive Liberty and Ethics, "A policy that deters students or bans them outright from participating in extracurricular activities isn't just bad for students, it's bad for society." Screening may simply decrease involvement in extracurriculars among students who have used drugs or even tried them once. Since the literature on juvenile delinquency clearly shows that the bulk of incidents occur between 3:00 and 6:00 P.M., we're simply decreasing the likelihood that students will engage in healthy activities and increasing the chance that they will do something less-good for them. Research has linked lack of participation in school activities to higher drop out rates, higher teen pregnancy rates, more likelihood of gang membership, and, who would have thought it—substance abuse!

The privacy of the test results remains in question.

Further, labeling kids as "druggies" or as "delinquents" can easily become a self-fulfilling prophecy. As Ronnie Casella explains in *At Zero Tolerance*, "the labels adults affix to students, including those denoting deviance, do more to justify maltreatment of young people than they do to treat students with the care and respect that they deserve." Since we know that it is extremely important to youth that they be respected by their peers as well as adults, labeling students based on the results of a highly flawed drug testing procedure may serve only to alienate and anger them.

Studies have shown that adolescent drug addiction is a developmental disorder. As adolescents develop, the motivational circuitry of their brains is changing, making them more vulnerable to the effects of alcohol and addictive drugs, according to Yale University School of Medicine researchers. This is not to say that we necessarily need to allow students to use drugs and alcohol, but we do need to try understanding, rather than alienating, in order to have any positive impact on their behavior.

Intimidation Doesn't Work

The continued use of intimidation tactics to ferret out drug users in schools is clearly not working and may be detrimental to kids. Even so-called educational programs like D.A.R.E. [Drug Abuse Resistance Education] are taught by police officers, not trained drug educators, and tend to be grounded in a threat-based approach; "if you use drugs, you will be a loser

... have no friends ... go to jail ... blah, blah, blah." Such methods of social control may lead us further down the road toward people simply assuming they have no privacy rights, as that is what they have become accustomed to. According to Boire, "Raised with the ever-present specter of coercion and control where urine testing is as common as standardized testing, today's students will have little if any privacy expectations when they reach adulthood." The real goal of drug testing and other school surveillance techniques may be just that; to desensitize future generations to civil rights abuses that prior generations would not have tolerated.

Particularly troubling is that drug testing, as with all the types of searches ..., sends the wrong message to students.

Particularly troubling is that drug testing, as with all the types of searches ..., sends the wrong message to students. Said one father at a school just beginning to drug test their athletes, "From my perspective, it's an insult. I find it very invasive and symptomatic of a social trend in this country where you are assumed guilty until you are proven innocent." Drug prevention efforts would likely be more effective if we were to try harder to base it on realistic information, rather than fear tactics. As Dr. Kent Holtorf, author of *Ur-Ine Trouble*, notes, all our efforts are based on the faulty "drug use equals drug abuse" premise. This is in contrast to what students actually see; they often know of many people who have used drugs, especially marijuana, without a problem. Since they know that nobody applies the same logic to alcohol use in our "alcohol-swilling society," the message that drug use equals abuse "is regarded as further evidence that the entire antidrug message is a pack of lies."

While alienating students, drug testing fails to serve any practical purpose in schools. First, it is terribly expensive, especially when the cost-per-catch is considered. Second, contrary to claims by politicians, it fails to deter use among any student group.... Finally, students in schools with testing report less belief that drug use has negative consequences and greater belief that it has benefits than do non-tested students. The bottom line: Drug testing in schools is a mess that can't be cleaned up.

8

Student Drug Testing Helps Prevent Drug Abuse

Office of National Drug Control Policy
Created by the Anti-Drug Abuse Act of 1988, the White House
Office of National Drug Control Policy establishes policies, pri-
orities, and objectives for the nation's drug control program.

Drug testing among student athletes and those students in extra-
curricular activities helps prevent drug abuse because the threat
of discovery discourages students from beginning drug use or en-
courages them to stop. By refraining from drug use, students
avoid negative cognitive consequences—the impairment of motor
skills, loss of memory, and detriments to critical thinking and
problem solving. Students are then better able to achieve aca-
demic success. Drug test results are confidential, and if drug use
is detected, students are not punished but encouraged to seek
treatment. Many students support drug testing because it pro-
vides a reason to say no when offered drugs. Ultimately, every-
one in the community benefits when the vicious cycle of drug
abuse is halted.

Thanks to advances in medical technology, researchers are now able to capture pictures of the human brain under the influence of drugs. As these images clearly show, the pleasurable sensations produced by some drugs are due to actual physical changes in the brain. Many of these changes are long-lasting, and some are irreversible. Scientists have recently dis-

The White House Office of National Drug Control Policy, "Drug Testing: An Overview," www.whitehousedrugpolicy.gov.

covered that the brain is not fully developed in early childhood, as was once believed, but is in fact still growing even in adolescence. Introducing chemical changes in the brain through the use of illegal drugs can therefore have far more serious adverse effects on adolescents than on adults.

Even so-called soft drugs can take a heavy toll. Marijuana's effects, for example, are not confined to the "high"; the drug can also cause serious problems with memory and learning, as well as difficulty in thinking and problem solving. Use of methamphetamine or Ecstasy (MDMA) may cause long-lasting damage to brain areas that are critical for thought and memory. In animal studies, researchers found that four days of exposure to Ecstasy caused damage that persisted for as long as six or seven years. Kids on drugs cannot perform as well in school as their drug-free peers of equal ability. So if testing reduces students' use of illicit drugs, it will remove a significant barrier to academic achievement. . . .

A Major Health Issue

Substance abuse should be recognized for what it is—a major health issue—and dealt with accordingly. Like vision and hearing tests, drug testing can alert parents to potential problems that continued drug use might cause, such as liver or lung damage, memory impairment, addiction, overdose, even death. Once the drug problem has been identified, intervention and then treatment, if appropriate, can begin.

Testing can also be an effective way to prevent drug use. The expectation that they may be randomly tested is enough to make some students stop using drugs—or never start in the first place.

That kind of deterrence has been demonstrated many times over in the American workplace. Employees in many national security and safety-sensitive positions—airline pilots, commercial truck drivers, school bus drivers, to name a few—are subject to pre-employment and random drug tests to ensure public safety. Employers who have followed the Federal model have seen a 67-percent drop in positive drug tests. Along with significant declines in absenteeism, accidents, and healthcare costs, they've also experienced dramatic increases in worker productivity.

If testing reduces students' use of illicit drugs, it will remove a significant barrier to academic achievement.

While some students resist the idea of drug testing, many endorse it. For one thing, it gives them a good excuse to say "no" to drugs. Peer pressure among young people can be a powerful and persuasive force. Knowing they may have to submit to a drug test can help kids overcome the pressure to take drugs by giving them a convenient "out." This could serve them well in years to come: Students represent the workforce of tomorrow, and eventually many will need to pass a drug test to get a job.

It is important to understand that the goal of school-based drug testing is not to punish students who use drugs. Although consequences for illegal drug use should be part of any testing program—suspension from an athletic activity or revoked parking privileges, for example—the primary purpose is to deter use and guide those who test positive into counseling or treatment. In addition, drug testing in schools should never be undertaken as a stand-alone response to the drug problem. Rather, it should be one component of a broader program designed to reduce students' use of illegal drugs.

The Benefits of Drug Testing

Drug use can quickly turn to dependence and addiction, trapping users in a vicious cycle that destroys families and ruins lives. Students who use drugs or alcohol are statistically more likely to drop out of school than their peers who don't. Dropouts, in turn, are more likely to be unemployed, to depend on the welfare system, and to commit crimes. If drug testing deters drug use, everyone benefits—students, their families, their schools, and their communities.

Drug and alcohol abuse not only interferes with a student's ability to learn, it also disrupts the orderly environment necessary for all students to succeed. Studies have shown that students who use drugs are more likely to bring guns and knives to school, and that the more marijuana a student smokes, the greater the chances he or she will be involved in physical attacks, property destruction, stealing, and cutting classes. Just as parents and students can expect schools to offer protection from violence, racism, and other forms of abuse, so do they have the right to expect a learning environment free from the influence of illegal drugs. . . .

A Case History: Hunterdon Central Regional High School

Teachers and administrators at Hunterdon Central Regional High School in Flemington, New Jersey, were alarmed. A survey taken during the 1996–1997 school year revealed that 45 percent of the school's 2,500 students had smoked marijuana, 70 percent were drinking alcohol, and 13 percent of all seniors had used cocaine. More than 10 percent of the student population had used hallucinogens, and 38 percent of seniors reported that heroin was readily available to them.

"Our drug problem was probably no worse than that of other high schools," says Principal Lisa Brady. "But for us, this was just unacceptable."

In September 1997, Hunterdon began a random drug-testing program for all student athletes. Urine was tested for marijuana, cocaine, heroin/codeine, amphetamine/metamphetamine, PCP, steroids, and alcohol. If a student tested positive, the school notified the parents and set up a meeting with the student, his or her parents, and a school counselor to discuss treatment options. The student attended a mandatory 4-week drug education course and was suspended from athletic activity until a subsequent test showed the drug use had stopped.

The expectation that they may be randomly tested is enough to make some students stop using drugs.

"We had one of the best random testing implementations in the country," says Brady. "It was working well." Indeed, a survey in 1999 showed that drug use at Hunterdon had declined in 20 of 28 key categories. For example, cocaine use among seniors had dropped from 13 percent to 4 percent, according to the survey. In another encouraging finding, the number of 10th graders reporting little or no use of drugs or alcohol increased from 41.8 percent to 47.3 percent.

Brady credits drug testing for the decline. "It was the only variable in the equation," she says. "Nothing else had changed." Hunterdon expanded its testing program in February 2000 to include students participating in any extracurricular activity. Even kids who wanted to act in school plays or obtain a parking permit could be called in to take a drug test. Eventually, problems with adulterated urine samples prompted school officials to give up urine testing and start testing oral fluids.

In September 2000, however, the school suspended all random testing when the American Civil Liberties Union filed a lawsuit in New Jersey state court on behalf of students who claimed their Fourth Amendment rights were violated. (The suit is still pending. [This case was closed in 2003 after the New Jersey Supreme Court ruled for the school's policy.]) Since the school halted testing, Brady has seen what she believes to be clear evidence that drug use at Hunterdon had begun to rise. "There's no question it's gotten worse," she says.

Before drug testing began at Hunterdon, many people in the community resisted the idea, explains Brady. "Now parents are demanding that we test their kids."

The Goals of Drug Testing

Again, the aim of drug testing is not to trap and punish students who use drugs. It is, in fact, counterproductive simply to punish them without trying to alter their behavior. If drug-using students are suspended or expelled without any attempt to change their ways, the community will be faced with drug-using dropouts, an even bigger problem in the long run. The purpose of testing, then, is to prevent drug dependence and to help drug-dependent students become drug free.

Before implementing a drug-testing program, parents and communities must make sure appropriate resources are in place to deal with students who test positive. For example, substance-abuse specialists should be available to determine the nature and extent of the drug use, and there should be comprehensive treatment services for students with potentially serious drug problems. Schools need to educate parents about exactly what the drug tests are measuring and what to do if their child tests positive. It is vital for parents to know that resources are available to help them gauge the extent of their child's drug use and, if necessary, find drug treatment.

For those who worry about the "Big Brother" dimension of drug testing, it is worth pointing out that test results are generally required by law to remain confidential, and in no case are they turned over to the police.

9

Student Drug Testing Has Not Been Proven to Prevent Drug Abuse

Oscar G. Bukstein

Oscar G. Bukstein is an associate professor of psychiatry at the University of Pittsburgh School of Medicine and is with the Western Psychiatric Institute and Clinic. He is board certified in Psychiatry and Child and Adolescent Psychiatry with an added qualification in Addiction Psychiatry. He has experience in the treatment of adolescents with substance abuse and psychiatric disorders.

Very little data supports the supposition that random drug testing of student athletes or those involved in extracurricular activities is an effective deterrent to student drug use. Specifically, evidence indicates that there is no difference in rates of drug use between schools that use drug testing and those that do not. While there may be some benefit in a drug testing program, there are problems as well. For example, high-risk students— those not involved in extracurricular activities—are not tested. In addition, the most common drug abused—alcohol—is not tested for. Finally, random drug testing is an invasion of student privacy. Until studies indicate otherwise, only those students clearly demonstrating a behavior associated with drug use should be tested.

Oscar G. Bukstein, "Drug Testing in Schools: Good Practice or Good Politics?" *Behavioral Health Management,* July/August 2004. Copyright © 2004 by Medquest Communications, LLC. Reproduced by permission.

Despite hundreds of millions of dollars of federal, state, local, and private funds spent to support drug-prevention programs, drug use among high school, and even middle school, students remains high. Often in desperation, secondary schools have turned to random drug testing as a potential aid in preventing illicit substance use or use disorders. "Random drug testing," in this context, is distinguished from school policies that require drug testing "for cause" or suspicion of use. Schools have used for-cause drug testing for years and usually follow carefully delineated procedures, often including parental consent. Random drug testing has been the subject of recent court decisions and is controversial.

Although the Supreme Court has ruled that the random testing of all students is unconstitutional, the Court recently held [in 2002] in a five-to-four decision that a mandatory drug-testing program for students involved in extracurricular activities is permissible (*Board of Education of Independent School District No. 92 of Pottawatomie County v. Earls*, 122 S.Ct. 2559 [2002]). The Court previously had ruled that student athletes could be tested (*Vernonia School District 47 J v. Acton*, 515 U.S. 646 [1995]). These decisions greatly expand the potential for school drug testing.

Few, if any, published data support the effectiveness of student drug testing.

Earlier [in 2004], the [George W.] Bush administration proposed to add $23 million to support school drug-testing programs. In fiscal year 2003, the Department of Education's Office of Safe and Drug-Free Schools awarded several million dollars in grants to schools around the country for demonstration projects of student drug-testing programs. Despite the concerns of some civil libertarians and the limitation of testing to students participating in extracurricular activities, much enthusiasm exists for implementing and expanding drug testing in many public and private schools.

Little Supporting Data

Unfortunately, little science and few data support the enthusiasm. While drug-testing programs have had some effect in decreasing drug use in the workplace and the military, few, if any, published data support the effectiveness of student drug testing, although John Walters, director of the White House Office of National Drug Control Policy (ONDCP), has stated that "testing has been shown to be extremely effective at reducing drug use in schools and businesses all over the country." Because until recently the constitutionality of random drug testing was uncertain, there has been little time to implement studies of its effectiveness. Now there is an assumption that random drug testing works. Before we either provide wholesale support for or condemnation of student drug testing, we should know the limited evidence for and against it, as well as consider the general pros and cons of this practice.

As part of the Monitoring the Future study, [Ryoko] Yamaguchi [a researcher at the University of Michigan] provided descriptive information on the drug testing conducted by schools participating in the study. Drug testing in these programs was not associated with the prevalence of self-reported illicit drug use or with the rate among experienced marijuana users. The investigators reported identical rates of drug use in schools with and without drug-testing policies, including random testing policies. Proponents of drug testing assert that the study's methodology was flawed, but the study, in fact, represents one of the best examples of science in this area, short of a randomized intervention trial.

[Linn] Goldberg [of the Oregon Health Sciences University] and associates compared two high schools, one with a policy of mandatory drug testing prior to sports participation and a control high school with no such policy. Although the high schools differed somewhat along racial/ethnic lines, self-report from athletes at the school with drug testing found lower 30-day illicit drug use and athletic-enhancing drug use than those from the control high school. Unfortunately, many risk factors associated with drug use—including norms of use, belief in lower risk of drugs, and poorer attitudes toward school—increased more among the student athletes at the school with drug testing than at the school without drug testing.

Because we can test students does not mean that we should.

The remaining "evidence" for the effectiveness of random drug testing includes anecdotes and unpublished surveys. Moreover, in the one study (Goldberg's) suggestive of a positive relationship between drug testing and decreased substance use, the authors expressed caution regarding the results and advised that larger studies, extending over several years, would have to be completed before student drug testing was supported by empirical evidence.

ONDCP suggests that schools tread carefully before implementing drug-testing policies or programs, advising school administrators to seek the advice and input of attorneys, parents, and teachers, as well as prevention and treatment professionals. Also recommended are policies that are not punitive but rather focus upon positive test results (confirmed by a second drug test) and mandate further evaluation and/or treatment. Expulsions or suspensions, says ONDCP, should be delivered only in cases of noncompliance with evaluation or treatment. Furthermore, drug testing should be only one component of a broader program, including prevention and treatment elements, designed to reduce student drug use.

Problems with Random Drug Testing

Clearly, drug testing has potential benefits, including reduced adolescent drug use and early identification for intervention. However, obstacles remain. At the moment, random drug testing is approved only for youth involved in athletics and other extracurricular activities, although these adolescents represent the lowest-risk youth for drug use and associated problems; thus, adolescents at highest risk will not be tested. Furthermore, drug testing does not yet include alcohol, still the most common "drug" of abuse. Risks of a random testing program include invasion of privacy with or without parental permission; costs of the program in terms of time, money, and other resources; potential violations of confidentiality; and creating a more adversarial environment between students and school staff. Although the ONDCP recommends development of procedures for referral to professionals for evaluation and possible treatment, schools cannot ensure that students who do not have health insurance will be able to access appropriate services or that those with health insurance will have access to benefits and providers offering what they need. In this era of decreasing budgets, resources that go to drug testing ($10 to $30 per test) may come at the expense of other resources, such as counselors and prevention programs, which research has shown to be highly effective.

Because we can test students does not mean that we should. From the federal government to professional societies, evidence-based practices are supported for both education and behavioral medicine, and random student drug testing without cause does not yet have evidence-based support. Therefore, prior to advocating widespread support or adoption of such drug-testing policies, federal and local governments should support rigorous controlled studies of student drug testing. Only when evidence of positive effects for student drug testing becomes available should adoption and funding of random drug-testing programs by governments and school districts be considered.

In the meantime, we should be supporting a more considered form of student drug testing—that for "cause or suspicion." Youth with drug problems almost always manifest a range of behavioral and emotional problems that are obvious to school staff, parents, and peers. Although this represents a distinct minority of high school students, these are the students who need to be tested and would be most helped by subsequent intervention. All students, particularly high-risk students, potentially could benefit from this approach to testing. Beyond this, government and school districts should continue to focus on evidence-based practices rather than politically expedient ones.

10

Student Drug Testing Is an Invasion of Privacy

Richard Glen Boire

Richard Glen Boire is the director and chief legal counsel of the Center for Cognitive Liberty and Ethics, an organization that seeks to protect and advance freedom of thought in an age of advancing technological development. In addition to authoring several books, his articles and essays have appeared in a variety of publications, and he has been a featured speaker at national and international conferences.

The 2002 Supreme Court decision to allow drug testing of all students who would like to participate in extracurricular activities is an attack on the Fourth Amendment to the U.S. Constitution, which guarantees a "reasonable expectation of privacy." The ruling means that students can be treated like suspects without exhibiting suspicious behavior. While the Court believes that drug testing will deter drug use, such testing may have an unwanted consequence. It may also deter those students who do not use drugs from participating in extracurricular activities because they do not want to submit to invasive testing procedures. Rather than resorting to failed scare tactics to deter student use of drugs, schools should instead institute education programs that will help those students who will inevitably experiment with drugs to minimize the risks they take.

The Supreme Court's ruling on June 27, 2002, giving public school authorities the green light to conduct random, suspicious drug testing of all junior and senior high school students wishing to participate in extracurricular activities, teaches by example. The lesson, unfortunately, is that the Fourth Amendment has become a historical artifact, a quaint relic from bygone days when our country honored the "scrupulous protection of constitutional freedoms of the individual . . . "[as the Court stated in a 1943 ruling.]

The Court's ruling turns logic on its head, giving the insides of students' bodies less protection than the insides of their backpacks, the contents of their bodily fluids less protection than the contents of their telephone calls. The decision elevates the myopic hysteria of a preposterous "zero-tolerance" drug war over basic values such as respect and dignity for our nation's young people.

The Court's ruling treats America's teenage students like suspects. If a student seeks to participate in after-school activities, his or her urine can be taken and tested for any reason or for no reason at all. Gone are any requirements for individualized suspicion. Trust and respect have been replaced with a generalized distrust—an accusatory, authoritarian demand that students prove their "innocence" at the whim of the schoolmaster.

The Court's Decision

The Court majority reasoned that requiring students to yield up their urine for examination as a prerequisite to participating in extracurricular activities would serve as a deterrent to drug use. It reasoned that students who seek to join the debate team, write for the student newspaper, play in the marching band, or participate in any other after-school activities would be dissuaded from using drugs knowing that their urine would be tested.

While some students may indeed be deterred from using drugs, the conventional wisdom (supported by empirical data) is that students who participate in extracurricular activities are some of the least likely to use drugs. Noting this, Justice Ruth Bader Ginsburg, whose dissenting opinion was joined by Justices John Paul Stevens, Sandra Day O'Connor, and David Souter, harshly condemned random testing of such students and describes it as "unreasonable, capricious and even perverse." Even when applied to students who do use drugs, the Court's decision merely makes matters worse.

The Failure of the "War on Drugs"

The federal government has tried everything from threatening imprisonment to yanking student loans to spending hundreds of millions of dollars on "just say no" advertisements, and still some students continue to experiment with marijuana and other drugs. Like it or not, some students will use illegal drugs before graduating from high school, just as some students will have sex. Perhaps it's time to rethink the wisdom of declaring a "war on drugs" and adopt instead a realistic and effective strategy more akin to safe-sex education.

The Fourth Amendment has become a historical artifact, a quaint relic from bygone days.

Ultimately, if a student does choose to experiment with an illegal drug (or a legal drug like alcohol), I suspect that many parents, like myself, would prefer that their child be taught the skills necessary to survive the experiment with as little harm as possible to self or others. The Drug Abuse Resistance Education (DARE) program—the nation's primary "drug education" curriculum—is taught by police officers, not drug experts, and is centered on intimidation and threats of criminal prosecution rather than on harm reduction. Random, suspicious urine testing fits the same tired mold.

Among the significant gaps in the majority's reasoning is its failure to consider the individual and social ramifications of deterring any student (whether or not they use drugs) from participating in after-school activities. Students who on principle prefer to keep their bodily fluids to themselves or who consider urine testing to be a gross invasion of privacy will be dissuaded from participating in after-school activities altogether. Similarly, students who do use drugs and who either test positive or forego the test for fear of what it might reveal will be banned from after-school activities and thus left to their own devices.

Extracurricular programs are valued for producing "well-rounded" students. Many adults look back on their extramural activities as some of the most educational, enriching, and formative experiences of their young lives. Extracurricular programs build citizenship, and for many universities participation in after-school clubs and academic teams is a decisive admissions criterion. Whether or not students use drugs, it makes no sense to bar them from the very activities that build citizenship and help prepare them for leadership roles in the workforce, or help them get into college. In other words, a policy that deters students or bans them outright from participating in extracurricular activities isn't just bad for students, it's bad for society.

A Constitutional Dark Age

Aside from eviscerating the Fourth Amendment rights of the nation's twenty-three million public school students and imposing a punishment that harms society as much at it harms students, the decision foreshadows a constitutional dark age. When a young person is told to urinate in a cup within earshot of a school authority listening intently, and then ordered to turn over his or her urine for chemical examination, what "reasonable expectation of privacy" remains? When today's students graduate and walk out the schoolhouse gates, what will become of society's "reasonable expectation of privacy"?

Raised with the ever present specter of coercion and control where urine testing is as common as standardized testing, today's students will have little if any privacy expectations when they reach adulthood. As a result, what society presently regards as a "reasonable expectation of privacy" will be considerably watered down within a single generation. Rivers of urine will have eroded the Fourth Amendment—our nation's strictest restraint on the overreaching and strong-arm tendencies of some government police agents. Justice Ginsburg and the three other justices who joined her dissenting opinion aptly state "that [schools] are educating the young for citizenship is reason for scrupulous protection of Constitutional freedoms of the individual, if we are not to strangle the free mind at its source and teach youth to discount important principles of our government as mere platitudes."

Treated as Enemies

The U.S. government has just allocated another $19 billion to fight the so-called war on drugs, yet all we really have to show for it is a tattered Constitution and the largest prison population in the history of the world. Fellow U.S. citizens have been constructed as "the enemy" simply because they'd rather have a puff of marijuana than a shot of bourbon. And that is perhaps the greatest tragedy of the Court's ruling. The decision not only victimizes our children, but it makes them the enemy. Being a public school student is now synonymous with being a criminal suspect or a prisoner.

Being a public school student is now synonymous with being a criminal suspect or a prisoner.

The values of trust and respect have been chased from the schoolyards and replaced with baseless suspicion and omnipresent policing. The lesson for U.S. students as they stand in line with urine bottles in hand is that the Fourth Amendment's guarantee is now a broken promise, yesterday's dusty trophy, and worthy only of lip service. The lesson for the rest of us is that the so-called war on drugs desperately needs rethinking.

11

Student Drug Testing Is Not an Invasion of Privacy

Clarence Thomas

Clarence Thomas is a member of the Supreme Court of the United States. He was sworn in by President George H.W. Bush in 1991 and has aligned himself with the conservative justices on the Court.

In the case of Board of Education of Independent School District No. 92 of Pottawatomie County et al., v. Lindsay Earls et al., *the U.S. Supreme Court finds that it is constitutional for the school district to conduct drug testing of all students participating in extracurricular activities. The students in the case believed that drug testing violated their Fourth Amendment right to reasonable search and seizure and that urine tests represented an invasion of privacy. However, the Court found that because drugs are a pervasive problem in American society and because drugs and drug paraphernalia were found at the school, it was reasonable for the school district to test students so as to preserve their health and safety. In particular, the Court stated that a student's expectation of privacy at school is limited—for example, they routinely submit to physical examinations and receive medical care. Those in extracurricular activities have even less of an expectation of privacy because they travel together outside of school boundaries. During testing, there is minimal intru-*

Clarence Thomas, majority opinion, *Board of Education of Independent School District No. 92 of Pottawatomie County et al., v. Lindsay Earls et al.,* U.S. Supreme Court, June 27, 2002.

siveness because students are allowed a closed stall when submitting a urine sample. Results of the urine tests are kept confidential. In essence, the school district's interest in preventing drug use at school justifies a minimal intrusion into the students' privacy, and it is, therefore, constitutional for the district to require drug tests for students participating in extracurricular activities.

The Student Activities Drug Testing Policy implemented by the Board of Education of Independent School District No. 92 of Pottawatomie County (School District) requires all students who participate in competitive extracurricular activities to submit to drug testing. Because this Policy reasonably serves the School District's important interest in detecting and preventing drug use among its students, we hold that it is constitutional.

A History of the Case

The city of Tecumseh, Oklahoma, is a rural community located approximately 40 miles southeast of Oklahoma City. The School District administers all Tecumseh public schools. In the fall of 1998, the School District adopted the Student Activities Drug Testing Policy, which requires all middle and high school students to consent to drug testing in order to participate in any extracurricular activity. In practice, the Policy has been applied only to competitive extracurricular activities sanctioned by the Oklahoma Secondary Schools Activities Association, such as the Academic Team, Future Farmers of America, Future Homemakers of America, band, choir, pom pon, cheerleading, and athletics. Under the Policy, students are required to take a drug test before participating in an extracurricular activity, must submit to random drug testing while participating in that activity, and must agree to be tested at any time upon reasonable suspicion. The urinalysis tests are designed to detect only the use of illegal drugs, in-

cluding amphetamines, marijuana, cocaine, opiates, and bar-
bituates, not medical conditions or the presence of authorized
prescription medications.

At the time of their suit, both respondents attended
Tecumseh High School. Respondent Lindsay Earls was a member of the show choir, the marching band, the Academic Team,
and the National Honor Society. Respondent Daniel James
sought to participate in the Academic Team. Together with
their parents, Earls and James brought [an] action against the
School District, challenging the Policy both on its face and as
applied to their participation in extracurricular activities.
They alleged that the Policy violates the Fourth Amendment
as incorporated by the Fourteenth Amendment and requested
injunctive and declarative relief. They also argued that the
School District failed to identify a special need for testing students who participate in extracurricular activities, and that the
"Drug Testing Policy neither addresses a proven problem nor
promises to bring any benefit to students or the school." . . .

Is the Policy Reasonable?

The Fourth Amendment to the United States Constitution
protects "the right of the people to be secure in their persons,
houses, papers, and effects, against unreasonable searches and
seizures." Searches by public school officials, such as the collection of urine samples, implicate Fourth Amendment interests. We must therefore review the School District's Policy for
"reasonableness," which is the touchstone of the constitutionality of a governmental search.

In the criminal context, reasonableness usually requires a
showing of probable cause. The probable-cause standard, however, [as the Court's previous rulings have stated,] "is pecu-
liarly related to criminal investigations" and may be unsuited
to determining the reasonableness of administrative searches
where the "Government seeks to *prevent* the development of
hazardous conditions." The Court has also held that a warrant

and finding of probable cause are unnecessary in the public school context because such requirements "'would unduly interfere with the maintenance of the swift and informal disciplinary procedures [that are] needed.'"

Given that the School District's Policy is not in any way related to the conduct of criminal investigations, respondents do not contend that the School District requires probable cause before testing students for drug use. Respondents instead argue that drug testing must be based at least on some level of individualized suspicion. It is true that we generally determine the reasonableness of a search by balancing the nature of the intrusion on the individual's privacy against the promotion of legitimate governmental interests. But we have long held that "the Fourth Amendment imposes no irreducible requirement of [individualized] suspicion." "In certain limited circumstances, [and that,] the Government's need to discover such latent or hidden conditions, or to prevent their development, is sufficiently compelling to justify the intrusion on privacy entailed by conducting such searches without any measure of individualized suspicion." Therefore, in the context of safety and administrative regulations, a search unsupported by probable cause may be reasonable "when 'special needs, beyond the normal need for law enforcement, make the warrant and probable-cause requirement impracticable.'"

A student's privacy interest is limited in a public school environment where the State is responsible for maintaining discipline, health, and safety.

Significantly, this Court has previously held that "special needs" inhere in the public school context. While schoolchildren do not shed their constitutional rights when they enter the schoolhouse, "Fourth Amendment rights . . . are different in public schools than elsewhere; the 'reasonableness' inquiry cannot disregard the schools' custodial and tutelary responsibility for children." In particular, a finding of individualized suspicion may not be necessary when a school conducts drug testing.

In *Vernonia*, this Court held that the suspicionless drug testing of athletes was constitutional. The Court, however, did not simply authorize all school drug testing, but rather conducted a fact-specific balancing of the intrusion on the children's Fourth Amendment rights against the promotion of legitimate governmental interests. Applying the principles of *Vernonia* to the somewhat different facts of this case, we conclude that Tecumseh's Policy is also constitutional.

A Limited Expectation of Privacy

We first consider the nature of the privacy interest allegedly compromised by the drug testing. As in *Vernonia*, the context of the public school environment serves as the backdrop for the analysis of the privacy interest at stake and the reasonableness of the drug testing policy in general. . . .

A student's privacy interest is limited in a public school environment where the State is responsible for maintaining discipline, health, and safety. Schoolchildren are routinely required to submit to physical examinations and vaccinations against disease. Securing order in the school environment sometimes requires that students be subjected to greater controls than those appropriate for adults.

Respondents argue that because children participating in nonathletic extracurricular activities are not subject to regular physicals and communal undress, they have a stronger expectation of privacy than the athletes tested in *Vernonia*. This distinction, however, was not essential to our decision in *Vernonia*, which depended primarily upon the school's custodial responsibility and authority.

In any event, students who participate in competitive extracurricular activities voluntarily subject themselves to many of the same intrusions on their privacy as do athletes. Some of these clubs and activities require occasional off-campus travel and communal undress. All of them have their own rules and requirements for participating students that do not apply to the student body as a whole. For example, each of the competitive extracurricular activities governed by the Policy must abide by the rules of the Oklahoma Secondary Schools Activities Association, and a faculty sponsor monitors the students for compliance with the various rules dictated by the clubs and activities. This regulation of extracurricular activities further diminishes the expectation of privacy among schoolchildren. ("Somewhat like adults who choose to participate in a closely regulated industry, students who voluntarily participate in school athletics have reason to expect intrusions upon normal rights and privileges, including privacy" [as stated in *Vernonia*]). We therefore conclude that the students affected by this Policy have a limited expectation of privacy.

Minimal Intrusiveness

Next, we consider the character of the intrusion imposed by the Policy. Urination is "an excretory function traditionally shielded by great privacy." But the "degree of intrusion" on one's privacy caused by collecting a urine sample "depends upon the manner in which production of the urine sample is monitored."

Under the Policy, a faculty monitor waits outside the closed restroom stall for the student to produce a sample and must "listen for the normal sounds of urination in order to guard against tampered specimens and to insure an accurate chain of custody." The monitor then pours the sample into two bottles that are sealed and placed into a mailing pouch along with a consent form signed by the student. This procedure is virtually identical to that reviewed in *Vernonia*, except that it additionally protects privacy by allowing male students to produce their samples behind a closed stall. Given that we considered the method of collection in *Vernonia* a "negligible" intrusion, the method here is even less problematic.

In addition, the Policy clearly requires that the test results be kept in confidential files separate from a student's other educational records and released to school personnel only on a "need to know" basis. Respondents nonetheless contend that the intrusion on students' privacy is significant because the Policy fails to protect effectively against the disclosure of confidential information and, specifically, that the school "has been careless in protecting that information: for example, the Choir teacher looked at students' prescription drug lists and left them where other students could see them." But the choir teacher is someone with a "need to know," because during off-campus trips she needs to know what medications are taken by her students. Even before the Policy was enacted the choir teacher had access to this information. In any event, there is no allegation that any other student did see such information. This one example of alleged carelessness hardly increases the character of the intrusion.

The test results are not turned over to any law enforcement authority.

Moreover, the test results are not turned over to any law enforcement authority. Nor do the test results here lead to the imposition of discipline or have any academic consequences. Rather, the only consequence of a failed drug test is to limit the student's privilege of participating in extracurricular activities. Indeed, a student may test positive for drugs twice and still be allowed to participate in extracurricular activities. After the first positive test, the school contacts the student's parent or guardian for a meeting. The student may continue to participate in the activity if within five days of the meeting the student shows proof of receiving drug counseling and submits to a second drug test in two weeks. For the second positive test, the student is suspended from participation in all extra-curricular activities for 14 days, must complete four hours of substance abuse counseling, and must submit to monthly drug tests. Only after a third positive test will the student be suspended from participating in any extracurricular activity for the remainder of the school year, or 88 school days, which-ever is longer.

Given the minimally intrusive nature of the sample collec-tion and the limited uses to which the test results are put, we conclude that the invasion of students' privacy is not signifi-cant.

The Need to Prevent and Deter Drug Use

Finally, this Court must consider the nature and immediacy of the government's concerns and the efficacy of the Policy in meeting them. This Court has already articulated in detail the importance of the governmental concern in preventing drug use by schoolchildren. The drug abuse problem among our Nation's youth has hardly abated since *Vernonia* was decided in 1995. In fact, evidence suggests that it has only grown worse. As in *Vernonia,* "the necessity for the State to act is magnified by the fact that this evil is being visited not just upon individuals at large, but upon children for whom it has undertaken a special responsibility of care and direction." The health and safety risks identified in *Vernonia* apply with equal force to Tecumseh's children. Indeed, the nationwide drug epi-demic makes the war against drugs a pressing concern in ev-ery school.

Additionally, the School District in this case has presented specific evidence of drug use at Tecumseh schools. Teachers testified that they had seen students who appeared to be un-der the influence of drugs and that they had heard students speaking openly about using drugs. A drug dog found mari-juana cigarettes near the school parking lot. Police officers once found drugs or drug paraphernalia in a car driven by a

Future Farmers of America member. And the school board president reported that people in the community were calling the board to discuss the "drug situation." We decline to second-guess the finding of the District Court that "viewing the evidence as a whole, it cannot be reasonably disputed that the [School District] was faced with a 'drug problem' when it adopted the Policy."

The invasion of students' privacy is not significant.

Respondents consider the proffered evidence insufficient and argue that there is no "real and immediate interest" to justify a policy of drug testing nonathletes. We have recognized, however, that "[a] demonstrated problem of drug abuse ... [is] not in all cases necessary to the validity of a testing regime," but that some showing does "shore up an assertion of special need for a suspicionless general search program." The School District has provided sufficient evidence to shore up the need for its drug testing program. . . .

Given the nationwide epidemic of drug use, and the evidence of increased drug use in Tecumseh schools, it was entirely reasonable for the School District to enact this particular drug testing policy. We reject the Court of Appeals' novel test that "any district seeking to impose a random suspicionless drug testing policy as a condition to participation in a school activity must demonstrate that there is some identifiable drug abuse problem among a sufficient number of those subject to the testing, such that testing that group of students will actually redress its drug problem." Among other problems, it would be difficult to administer such a test. As we cannot articulate a threshold level of drug use that would suffice to justify a drug testing program for schoolchildren, we refuse to fashion what would in effect be a constitutional quantum of drug use necessary to show a "drug problem."

Respondents also argue that the testing of nonathletes does not implicate any safety concerns, and that safety is a "crucial factor" in applying the special needs framework. They contend that there must be "surpassing safety interests," or "extraordinary safety and national security hazards," in order to override the usual protections of the Fourth Amendment. Respondents are correct that safety factors into the special needs analysis, but the safety interest furthered by drug testing is undoubtedly substantial for all children, athletes and non-athletes alike. We know all too well that drug use carries a variety of health risks for children, including death from overdose.

Testing students . . . is a reasonably effective means of addressing the School District's legitimate concerns in preventing, deterring, and detecting drug use.

We also reject respondents' argument that drug testing must presumptively be based upon an individualized reasonable suspicion of wrongdoing because such a testing regime would be less intrusive. In this context, the Fourth Amendment does not require a finding of individualized suspicion, and we decline to impose such a requirement on schools attempting to prevent and detect drug use by students. Moreover, we question whether testing based on individualized suspicion in fact would be less intrusive. Such a regime would place an additional burden on public school teachers who are already tasked with the difficult job of maintaining order and discipline. A program of individualized suspicion might unfairly target members of unpopular groups. The fear of lawsuits resulting from such targeted searches may chill enforcement of the program, rendering it ineffective in combating drug use. In any case, this Court has repeatedly stated that reasonableness under the Fourth Amendment does not require employing the least intrusive means, because "the logic of such elaborate less-restrictive-alternative arguments could raise insuperable barriers to the exercise of virtually all search-and-seizure powers."

Finally, we find that testing students who participate in extracurricular activities is a reasonably effective means of addressing the School District's legitimate concerns in preventing, deterring, and detecting drug use. While in *Vernonia* there might have been a closer fit between the testing of athletes and the trial court's finding that the drug problem was "fueled by the 'role model' effect of athletes' drug use," such a finding was not essential to the holding. *Vernonia* did not require the school to test the group of students most likely to use drugs, but rather considered the constitutionality of the program in the context of the public school's custodial responsibilities. Evaluating the Policy in this context, we conclude that the drug testing of Tecumseh students who participate in extracurricular activities effectively serves the School District's interest in protecting the safety and health of its students.

Within the limits of the Fourth Amendment, local school boards must assess the desirability of drug testing schoolchildren. In upholding the constitutionality of the Policy, we express no opinion as to its wisdom. Rather, we hold only that Tecumseh's Policy is a reasonable means of furthering the School District's important interest in preventing and deterring drug use among its schoolchildren. Accordingly, we reverse the judgment of the Court of Appeals.

It is so ordered.

12

There Are Better Alternatives to Student Drug Testing

Fatema Gunja et al.

Fatema Gunja is the director of the Drug Policy Forum of Massachusetts, a statewide nonprofit organization working to reduce the harms associated with illegal drug use and current drug laws. She previously served as the communications coordinator of the American Civil Liberties Union Drug Policy Litigation Project. Marsha Rosenbaum is on staff with Drug Policy Alliance, an organization seeking alternative methods of fighting the war on drugs. Judith Appel and Alexandra Cox work for the Office of Legal Affairs for Drug Policy Alliance.

Drug testing is not an effective way to prevent student drug use and may inhibit school officials from noticing other signs of drug abuse. If a school implements a drug testing program, it may find unintended consequences. For example, students may turn to more dangerous drugs or to alcohol because the school may not test for them; students may employ methods of avoiding detection such as obtaining replacement urine or shaving their hair; also, students will learn that they do not have an expectation of privacy in their school life. Instead of employing a drug testing program, schools should use other deterrents. For instance, getting students involved in extracurricular activities, which leaves less time for drug use. Also, by providing counseling services, schools can build a relationship with teens and teach them about drugs. Lastly, students should be taught factual information about drug use through science-based classes so that they may make informed decisions throughout their lives.

Drug testing says very little about who is misusing or abusing drugs. Hundreds or even thousands of students might be tested in order to detect a tiny fraction of students who may have used the drugs covered by the test. Additionally, students misusing other harmful substances not detected by drug tests will not be identified. If schools rely on drug testing, they may undervalue better ways of detecting young people who are having problems with drugs. Most often, problematic drug use is discovered by learning to recognize its common symptoms. Teachers, coaches, and other school officials can identify students with a drug problem by paying attention to such signs as student absences, erratic behavior, changes in grades, and withdrawal from peers.

Drug Testing Has Unintended Consequences

Students may turn to more dangerous drugs or binge drinking. Because marijuana is the most detectable drug, students may switch to drugs they think the test will not detect, like Ecstasy (MDMA) or inhalants. Knowing alcohol is less detectable, they may also engage in binge drinking, creating greater health and safety risks for students and the community as a whole.

Students can outsmart the drug test. Students who fear being caught by a drug test may find ways to cheat the test, often by purchasing products on the Internet. A quick search on the Internet for "passing a drug test" yields over 8,000 hits, linking students to web sites selling drug-free replacement urine, herbal detoxifiers, hair follicle shampoo, and other products designed to beat the drug test. In addition, a new subculture of students might emerge that makes a mockery of the drug testing program. For example, in one school district in Louisiana, students who were facing a hair test shaved their heads and body hair.

Students learn that they are guilty until proven innocent. Students are taught that under the U.S. Constitution, people are presumed innocent until proven guilty and that they have a reasonable expectation of privacy. Random drug testing undermines both lessons; students are assumed guilty until they can produce a clean urine sample, with little regard given to students' privacy rights.

Alternatives to Student Drug Testing

The current push to increase drug testing comes from the drug testing industry, but also from well-intentioned educators and parents frustrated by the lack of success of drug prevention programs such as Drug Abuse Resistance Education (DARE). However, there are more effective ways to keep teens out of trouble with drugs.

Engage students in after school programs. Schools and local communities should help engage students in extracurricular activities and athletics since these are among the best deterrents for drug misuse.

Incorporate reality-based drug education into the school curriculum. Drugs of all sorts abound in our society. We are constantly confronted with a wide variety of substances that have recreational and medicinal uses and that can be purchased over the counter, by prescription, and illegally. Since decisions to use drugs of all kinds is ongoing, quality drug education should be incorporated into a broad range of science classes, including physiology, chemistry, and biology, as well as psychology, history, and sociology. Drug education should avoid dishonest scare tactics, and it should also recognize the wide spectrum of drug use and misuse, and the reasons why young people might choose to use (or not use) drugs.

Provide counseling. Schools should provide counseling for students who are using drugs in a way that is causing harm to themselves or others. An emerging model, which stresses relationships between students and counselors, is that of a comprehensive Student Assistance Program (SAP). Both prevention education and intervention can occur in such a program. Counselors who teach about drugs can remain an important resource for students after the formal session ends. Trained student counselors can engage students who may feel more comfortable talking about their problems with their peers.

If schools rely on drug testing, they may undervalue better ways of detecting young people who are having problems with drugs.

Allow students to be assessed and treated by health care professionals. Schools can refer students to health care professionals who can play a role in screening, intervening, and referring adolescents to treatment. Several screening tools, other than urinalysis, such as questionnaires, are available to health care professionals in diagnosing drug abuse among adolescents.

Encourage parents to become better informed. Informed parents play a key role in preventing and detecting drug misuse, so they should learn as much as they can. Schools can encourage parents to open a dialogue when adolescents are actually confronted with alcohol and other intoxicating drugs, usually in middle school. At this point, "drug talks" should be two-way conversations. It is important for parents to teach as well as learn from their children.

Cultivate trust and respect among students and adults. Trust and respect are perhaps the most important elements of a relationship with teens. Young people who have the confidence of their parents and teachers, and are expected to assume responsibility for their actions, are the most likely, in turn, to act responsibly. They need to practice responsibility while still in high school where they have a parental and school "safety net."

The combination of these methods will help ensure that students:

1. Receive comprehensive, science-based information;

2. receive help when they need it; and

3. stay busy and involved in productive activities when the school day ends.

Organizations to Contact

American Civil Liberties Union (ACLU)
125 Broad St., 18th Fl., New York, NY   10004
(212) 549-2585
Web site: www.aclu.org

The ACLU works in courts, legislatures, and communities to defend and preserve the individual rights and liberties guaranteed by the Constitution and laws of the United States. Its Web page on drug testing provides press releases, legal documents, fact sheets, and resource information.

American Council for Drug Education (ACDE)
164 W. Seventy-fourth St., New York, NY   10023
(800) 488-DRUG (3784)
e-mail: acde@phoenixhouse.org
Web site: www.acde.org

The ACDE is a substance abuse prevention and education agency that develops programs and materials based on the most current scientific research on drug use and its impact on society. The organization's Web site offers information for parents, schools, and workplaces on drug detection, prevention, and support. It offers brochures, books, videos, and other publications on research, as well as information about drugs and alcohol.

Drug Abuse Resistance Education (D.A.R.E.)
9800 La Cienega Blvd., Suite 401, Inglewood, CA   90301
(800) 223-DARE (3273) • fax: (310) 215-0180
Web site: www.dare.com

D.A.R.E. is a drug abuse prevention education program designed to equip elementary, middle, and high school children with knowledge about drug abuse, the consequences of abuse, and skills for resisting peer pressure to experiment with drugs, alcohol, and tobacco. The D.A.R.E. Web site offers a curriculum and brochures on the program, advice for parents on preventing drug use, and news on drug use–related studies and government action.

The Drug and Alcohol Testing Industry Association (DATIA)
1600 Duke St., Suite 400, Alexandria, VA   22314
(800) 355-1257 • fax: (703) 519-1716
e-mail: DATIA@wpa.org
Web site: www.datia.org

DATIA represents the drug and alcohol testing industry in Washington, D.C., on key legislative and regulatory issues. It works to expand the workplace drug and alcohol testing market and provides members with information, resources, and benefits. Its Web site provides news, industry standards, and links to other industry sites. It publishes the *Drug Testing News,* which reports on the drug and alcohol testing industry, including legislation, legal issues, business, and technology.

Drug Policy Alliance
925 Fifteenth St. NW, 2nd Fl., Washington, DC   20005
(202) 216-0035 • fax: (202) 216-0803
e-mail: dc@drugpolicy.org
Web site: www.drugpolicy.org

The Drug Policy Alliance is an organization promoting alternatives to the use of scare tactics to inform the public—especially young people—about drug abuse. The alliance launched the Safety First program, which promotes education with science-based information for parents and teens. Its Web site offers the latest news, research studies, and legislative action related to drugs and drug testing, as well as links to other sites. The alliance also provides the largest online collection of journal articles, reports, books, testimonies, and fact sheets that focus on drugs and drug policy from economic, criminal justice, and public health perspectives.

The National Workrights Institute

166 Wall St., Princeton, NJ   08540
(609) 683-0313
e-mail: info@workrights.org
Web site: www.workrights.org/issue_drugtest.html

The institute works to improve the legal protection of human rights in the workplace. It does this by selecting a small number of issues, one of which is drug testing, where it believes it can make long-range improvement in workplace human rights. The organization's stated position is that employers have the right to expect workers not to be under the influence of drugs or alcohol on the job, but that they should not have the right to require all employees to take a drug test. Its Web page on drug testing offers a legal guide for public employees, a legislative brief, and news and information regarding drug testing and other issues in the workplace.

Office of National Drug Control Policy (ONDCP)

Drug Policy Information Clearinghouse
   Rockville, MD   20849-6000
(800) 666-3332 • fax: (301) 519-5212
e-mail: ondcp@ncjrs.org
Web site: www.whitehousedrugpolicy.gov

Established by the Anti–Drug Abuse Act of 1988, the ONDCP institutes policies, priorities, and objectives for the nation's drug control program, seeking to reduce illicit drug use, manufacturing, and trafficking; drug-related crime and violence; and drug-related health consequences. Its Web site provides fact sheets on research and drug-related topics, information about prevention and treatment programs, and an outline of law enforcement efforts in the United States and abroad. Its publications include *The Economic Costs of Drug Abuse in the United States, 1992–2002* and *Marijuana Myths & Facts: The Truth Behind 10 Popular Misperceptions.*

Student Drug-Testing Coalition

e-mail: mattf@rrohio.com

Web site: www.studentdrugtesting.org

The coalition is an international volunteer organization consisting of leaders of drug-prevention organizations and concerned parents who believe that nonpunitive student drug testing programs are the most effective and economical means to reduce student drug use. The Web site provides technical resources and factual information about student drug testing programs, including current research data on student drug testing and student drug use, student drug testing court case rulings, summaries of school policies, and links to other resources.

U.S. Department of Health and Human Services and SAMHSA's National Clearinghouse for Alcohol and Drug Information (NCADI)

11420 Rockville Pike, Rockville, MD   20852
(800) 729-6686 • fax: (301) 468-6433
Web site: http://ncadi.samhsa.gov

NCADI is a resource for information about substance abuse prevention and addiction treatment. NCADI also distributes a wide range of free or low-cost materials, including fact sheets, brochures, pamphlets, monographs, posters, and videotapes. Some of the brochures available include *Tips for Teens: The Truth About Marijuana* and *Mind over Matter: The Brain's Response to Methamphetamine.* Its personnel can perform customized searches for information in the form of annotated bibliographies and can also recommend publications.

World Anti-Doping Agency (WADA)

800 Place Victoria, Suite 1700, Montreal, Quebec
   Canada   H4Z 1B7
(514) 904-9232 • fax (514) 904-8650
e-mail: info@wada-ama.org
Web site: www.wada-ama.org

WADA is an independent foundation created in November 1999 to promote and coordinate the fight against doping in sport internationally through education, research, and the monitoring of athletes. Its Web site includes the International Standard for Testing, information about dietary supplements, and an athlete's guide to prohibited and exempt drugs. WADA also publishes *Play True* magazine.

Bibliography

Books

Michael S. Bahrke and Charles E. Yesalis, eds. *Performance-Enhancing Substances in Sport and Exercise.* Champaign, IL: Human Kinetics, 2002.

Joel B. Bennett *Preventing Workplace Substance Abuse: Beyond Drug Testing to Wellness.* Washington, DC: American Psychological Association, 2003.

James R. Brunet *Drug Testing in Law Enforcement Agencies: Social Control in the Public Sector.* New York: LFB, 2005.

Jim Kelaher *Drug Testing and the Workplace.* Philadelphia: Xlibris, 2004.

Mikki Norris, Chris Conrad, and Virginia Resner *Human Rights and the U.S. Drug War.* El Cerrito, CA: Creative Xpressions, 2001.

Charles J. Russo and Ralph D. Mawdsley *Searches, Seizures and Drug Testing Procedures: Balancing Rights and School Safety.* Horsham, PA: LRP, 2004.

Kenneth D. Tunnell *Pissing on Demand: Workplace Drug Testing and the Rise of the Detox Industry.* New York: New York University Press, 2004.

Wayne Wilson and Edward Derse, eds. — *Doping in Elite Sport: The Politics of Drugs in the Olympic Movement.* Champaign, IL: Human Kinetics, 2001.

Periodicals

Teresa Anderson — "Drug Testing: U.S. Judicial Decisions," *American Society for Industrial Security,* April 1, 2005.

Randall R. Beger — "The 'Worst of Both Worlds': School Security and the Disappearing Fourth Amendment Rights of Students," *Criminal Justice Review,* Autumn 2003.

Norm Brodsky — "Street Smarts: Just Say Yes," *Inc.,* November 1, 2004.

David Cohen — "Cheating Is Easier than You Think: Steroids Boost Performance in Just Three Weeks. That Might Explain How Some Athletes Dodge Drug Tests," *New Scientist,* August 14, 2004.

Kathy Dunn and Steven King — "Should Students Have to Take Drug Tests to Participate in Extracurricular Activities?" *NEA Today,* January 2005.

John Gehring — "Sports," *Education Week,* January 22, 2003.

Ruth Bader
Ginsburg

"Don't Expand Drug Tests in Schools," *Seattle Post-Intelligencer,* July 10, 2002.

Jerry Gjesvold

"Drug Testing Criteria Should Be Narrower," *Eugene Register-Guard,* April 20, 2002.

Lawrence O.
Gostin

"The Rights of Pregnant Women: The Supreme Court and Drug Testing," *Hastings Center Report,* September 1, 2001.

Julie Griffiths

"Negative Result for Work Drug Testing," *People Management,* June 30, 2004.

Lori Harrison-
Stone

"Safety Trumps Privacy in Employee Drug Testing Debates," *Arkansas Business,* March 24, 2003.

Linda Jacobson

"Supreme Court Allows Expansion of Schools' Drug-Testing Policies," *Education Week,* July 10, 2002.

Mary Clare
Jalonick

"Are Stronger Anti-Doping Policies Needed?" *CQ Researcher,* July 23, 2003.

Jessica King

"Drug Testing Infringes on Our Personal Rights," *America's Intelligence Wire,* November 21, 2002.

Jere Longman

"Drugs in Sports Creating Games of Illusion," *New York Times,* November 18, 2003.

Lance C. Presley — "Alternative Drug Testing Update," *Occupational Health & Safety,* January 31, 2003.

Dennis Reardon — "Small Companies Less Likely to Drug Test," *Central Penn Business Journal,* December 5, 2003.

Nina Riccio — "To Test or Not to Test? Random Drug Testing: Is It a Valuable Tool or a Personal Violation?" *Current Health,* March 2003.

Leah B. Rorvig — "Students Find Dialogue More Effective than Drug Testing," *USA Today,* February 2, 2004.

Marsha Rosenbaum — "Random Student Drug Testing Is No Panacea," *Alcoholism & Drug Abuse Weekly,* April 12, 2004.

Richard A. Samp — "Fighting Substance Abuse on Campus; School's Need to Safeguard Kids Outweighs Their Rights to Privacy from Searching," *Los Angeles Daily Journal,* April 12, 2002.

Tommy Santora — "Drug Testing Places Business in a Delicate Balance of Trust," *Kansas City (Mo.) Daily Record,* January 28, 2005.

Debra J. Saunders — "Want to Join the Chess Club? Pee in a Cup," *San Francisco Chronicle,* July 4, 2002.

Amy Shipley   "Amid Progress, Drug-Testing Still
                       Produces Mixed Results," *Washington
                       Post*, March 20, 2002.

Jacob Sullum   "Let the Love Flow: Student Drug
                       Testing," *Reason*, May 2004.

Jacob Sullum   "Urine—or You're Out: Drug Testing
                       Is Invasive, Insulting, and Generally
                       Irrelevant to Job Performance. Why
                       Do So Many Companies Insist on
                       It?" *Reason*, November 2002.

Clarence Thomas   "Equal Time: Policy Offers Reason-
                       able Way to Deter Students' Drug
                       Use," *Atlanta Journal-Constitution*,
                       May 29, 2003.

Tom Verducci   "Five Strikes and You're Out," *Sports
                       Illustrated*, November 24, 2003.

Index